on Pottery
and Porcelain

Mary Rogers

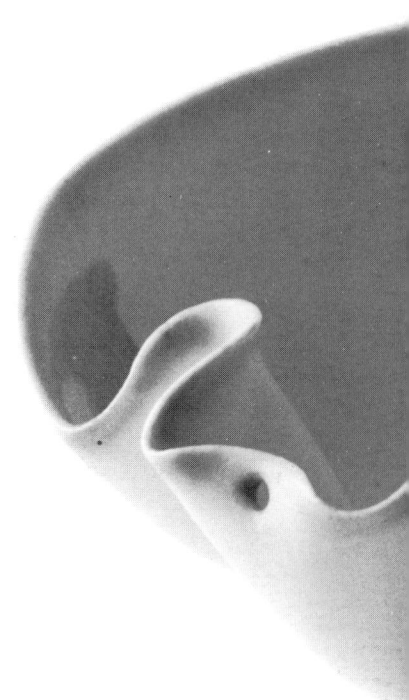

Watson-Guptill Publications, New York

on Pottery
and Porcelain

Alphabooks, England

Copyright © 1979 by Mary Rogers

This book was designed and produced by Alphabet and Image, Sherborne, Dorset, England

First published in England in 1979 by Alphabooks, Sherborne, Dorset, England

ISBN 0 9506171 3 X

First published 1979 in The United States by Watson-Guptill Publications, a division of Billboard Publications, Inc., 1515 Broadway, New York, N.Y. 10036

Library of Congress Cataloging in Publication Data

Rogers, Mary, 1929–
      Mary Rogers on pottery and porcelain.

      1. Rogers, Mary, 1929–   2. Pottery—Technique.
3. Porcelain—Technique.   I. Title   II. Title: On pottery and porcelain.
NK4210.R54A4   1979   738.1'4   79-1070
ISBN 0-8230-3011-3

Filmset and printed by BAS Printers Limited, Over Wallop, Hampshire, England and bound in Great Britain

Contents

Acknowledgments

I wish to express my gratitude to the following people: my husband, Bob (L. R.) Rogers, for his untiring encouragement and advice, for his help in reading the text, and for having taken the working photographs; Eric Webster, for his enthusiasm for the project, which has led to such sensitive photographic interpretations of the natural forms and of my work; Tony Birks for having suggested that I should write the book, and for the careful way in which he has made the book take shape; my brother, John Henley, for the photographs (page 119) taken in Africa during his work there on Intermediate Technology, and for reading and discussing Chapter 4 of the book with me; Sylvia Leith-Ross for allowing me to reproduce the African pots and their descriptions (pages 115–17, 122, 127, 128, 137) from her book on Nigerian Pottery, which is also the catalogue of the pottery collection at the Jos Museum, Nigeria; Michael O'Brien for the photographs (pages 120, 121, 130, 131 lower) which he has let me use from his article in *Ceramic Review* in 1975, and also for those taken in 1978, by Danlami Aliyu (pages 123, 126, 129, 131 top, 132); Giselle Underhill for the use of some of the photographs from her article in *Ceramic Review* in 1972 (pages 124–5); The Crafts Advisory Committee for photographs of the ceramics of Jill Crowley, Elizabeth Fritsch, and John Ward; Paul Koster for the photographs of the work of Ruth Duckworth (page 143); Peter Simpson and Sheila Fournier for sending me photographs of their work; the Trustees of the Victoria and Albert Museum for the photographs on pages 11, 134, 141; Patricia Searle and the Trustees of the British Museum (Natural History) for the photographs on page 14; Heather Angel for page 32; Natural History Photographic Agency for page 33; Collection, The Museum of Modern Art, New York, for Meret Oppenheim's 'Object' (Le Dejeuner en Fourrure) (1936), a photograph of which appears on page 60; Faber & Faber for the photographs on page 82 from *Japanese Pottery* by Soame Jenyns; and the Trustees of the British Museum for the photograph of the mosaic glass bowl on page 106.

List of colour plates

A handbuilder's approach

Described very simply, the way to make a pot by pinch-building is just to hold a lump of plastic clay in one hand, and then to push a hole into it with the fingers or thumb of the other hand. This will make a crude hollow form, a container, a bowl, a cup. In size and shape it will correspond to the hollow of the cupped hand or hands in which it has been made. It is possible that we unconsciously assess all constructed bowl shapes by this known hollow, the form within the cupped hands, which is our most basic container and drinking cup. I feel that this may also be the main reason why most people respond very immediately to simple pots made within the cradle of the hands. They correspond to a basic human body-shape or hollow, and so they have a comfortable familiarity and 'rightness' of size and shape; they line the inner curve of the hands and nestle within them.

Pinch-building was probably the first way in which a pot was made from clay. It is almost instinctive when holding a ball of soft clay in the hands to push your thumb into it, and then to turn it around whilst continuing to squeeze the sides, and so to form a simple hollowed-out shape. But this extreme simplicity of making does not mean that the results need necessarily be primitive and crude. The methods may be elementary but the resulting pots may be either simple and homely or highly refined and sophisticated. To take an analogy, it is a very simple activity to walk, and even to prance about a bit and dance when excited. But it needs great concentration and application to be able to dance beautifully and gracefully, and yet even more to do so expressively and with originality. And then, of course, there is the additional factor of having inherited the muscles, temperament, and build and balance of the body required for dancing really well. In the same way there are inevitably some people for whom hand-building is a more natural or suitable way of working than for others. But even for them it does need concentrated practice before it can be used as a worthwhile method of expression.

Possibly the type of mental approach needed to succeed with pinch-building suits some personalities rather than others. With hand-building in general, and especially with pinch-building, the maker must be happy to work slowly, quietly and patiently, without the quicker body rhythms and greater output of pieces possible with work on the wheel.

Making pottery by hand without a wheel usually leads to a heightened awareness of natural forms, since the method inevitably gives organic and somewhat asymmetrical effects similar to those of naturally growing forms. This may be why so many hand-builders, including myself, find themselves turning to natural forms as a source of inspiration. One becomes more and more

9

observant of the infinite subtleties, refinements and varieties of form and colour that there are in the natural world. This expanding awareness is probably its own justification, whatever the effects may be on the work. Even so, close observation of nature is sure to add immeasurably to the vocabulary of forms and colours used when actually working, so that each piece may become richer and more full of depth and interest. Besides this, you align yourself with a universal experience, because man has always tried to understand and form a relationship with the natural world by recording parts of its beauty in paint, clay, stone, story-telling, poetry, music, mime and dance.

The nature of clay itself as a material and the demands that it makes on potters probably also have some influence on their attitudes to work and to the world.

The basic material with which potters work bears little or no resemblance to the material of our final products. With a material whose malleability is its most valuable working characteristic, we make pots which are hard, rigid and immutable. We may design with the qualities of the finished fired clays in mind, but we do the actual making with a material which has none of these qualities.

Before being irreversibly fixed in its shape and physical state by firing, clay has a 'life cycle' of changing qualities. We have to get to know these before we can plan to make anything at all in clay.

All clays which are exposed to the air dry out. This is obvious, but the gradual loss of plasticity which it entails provides a series of predictable stages which can be anticipated and planned for in the growth of the piece. The 'life cycle' of the clay progresses inexorably from a wet and sticky mud, through a plastic stage to a leather-hard stage, and on to a material as rigid as stone. Fire may then be used permanently to harden this final form, or water may dissolve it back again to mud, and so start the cycle over again.

Useful work can be done at the muddy, sticky stage. It is a good time to prepare the clay, modifying it so that it will be suitable for the work we want to do with it when it is a little drier. Other clays and grogs will mix into it easily at this stage and, as the stickiness goes, wedging will help to even out the texture, and blend in any additional ingredients. This should give us the kind of clay that everyone enjoys working with—a plastic clay which is malleable and responsive to even the slightest pressure and coaxing, yet which will hold whatever shape it is given without slumping, spreading or splitting. I sometimes think that some of us go through all the other stages of mixing, weighing, glazing, kiln-packing and firing just to get round again to the tactile delight of actually handling the clay at this stage.

At the leather-hard stage the clay is still damp and slightly flexible. To some extent it can still be worked on, beaten into a better shape if necessary, carved as though it were a soft wood, scraped to remove unwanted thicknesses, burnished on the edges to remove any sharpnesses, or completely burnished all over to give a tighter surface, a shine and a deeper, richer colour after firing.

When dry and inflexible, clay is like a very

The raw material and the finished work. LEFT *The formless lump of clay.* BELOW *A Sung vase of the eleventh or twelfth century, stoneware with cream-white glaze: product of hand and mind.*

fragile and brittle soft stone. It can be worked by carving, scraping and abrading, that is by methods allied to those of stone sculpture, but it has to be treated with great care.

Occasionally I take a lump of clay, formless, dull coloured, and unable to fulfil any of the functions which ceramics can have, but simply a lump of mud, and I put it by a finished pot and realize that, not long ago, that pot was mud. It can be a miraculous transformation, a phoenix from the fire, especially if you make this comparison between unformed, undecorated, unfired clay, and some of the loveliest pots from the past.

The gradual but complete alteration of the nature of the material as we work with it—a process which our handling actually hastens—is, I think, peculiar to clay-working as a craft. It may make some of us more receptive to attitudes and philosophies of acceptance. Certainly societies in the past which have exalted ceramics to a high art-form—China, Korea, Japan—have lived by the tenets of Taoism or Zen Buddhism, which extol this attitude together with a contemplative respect for the natural world. This is mere speculation, but it is certainly true that

working with clay in a sensitive way can make us aware of the alteration in form which is the visible and tactile evidence of time passing.

There is a natural order governing change

and decay besides that which determines the forms of growth. Living things emerge, enlarge and diminish in a structured fashion, changing all the while in response to internal and external forces which dry out and wear away the softer living parts, and finally leave only the hard skeletal supports, bones, carapaces, shells and husks as a record of life. Nothing whilst it is growing or decaying lacks form, unity, pattern and order, unless it is diseased—de-formed as we graphically say. If we keep plants we know this and will notice when a leaf is not the right shape or tension. It is not necessarily perfect symmetry that we look for, but directional rhythm, unity of growth, fullness of form and regularity of pattern.

Besides the alteration inevitable during the span of life, external forces such as wind, water, fire, frost and sun all play on natural objects and can alter their shapes, either permanently or temporarily. They can erode away parts forever or produce secondary passing effects such as the patterns of wind amongst grasses, in clouds, or on water. These transitory variations can be thought of as the decoration or texture on a form.

With the modern developments of photography we have now become aware of a whole new world of shapes and patterns which were formerly either too minute, too huge, or else inaccessible to us by their existence in another element. The revelations which the photographer and scientist have given to us have added enormously to the fund from which we are able to draw our ideas, and to the associations which a piece may then suggest. For example, for the first time in history we know what the world looks like from outer space, the visual resemblance of a spiral nebulae to a shell, and the beautifully varied and intricate structure of radiolaria. We can

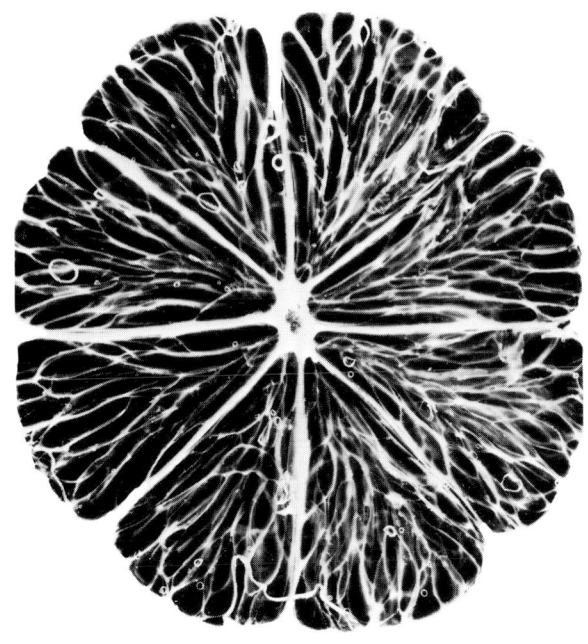

LEFT *When a lemon is full of juice the structure is filled out to capacity, giving a rich shape to the ripe fruit. As the lemon dries out* OPPOSITE *and the juice diminishes, the structure becomes evident but the nature of the form changes. As the green pepper* BELOW *ages and dies, the thick flexible skin wrinkles like a deflating balloon.*

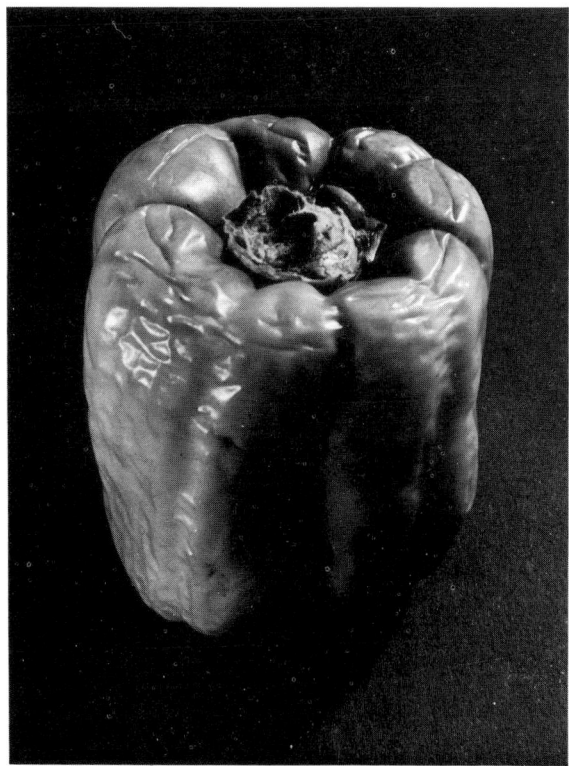

As size diminishes in nature new and often unexpected patterns are to be found. Thanks to the scanning electron microscope, tiny organisms and their substructures can be studied, magnified hundreds and thousands of times. BELOW *foraminifera, globigerina and micro-fossils from deep sea sediments. The pinched porcelain form* RIGHT *shares common elements of design with biological and sub-cellular structures. 4 inches diameter, 1972.*

now actually see slow processes of growth happening as though they were a rhythmic dance when speeded up on a film, and study the patterns of the wing-beats of an insect, which in reality move so quickly that they appear as just a formless blur to the naked eye. The magnification of things that are microscopic, the diminution of those that are immense, the slowing down of instantaneous occurrences, and the speeding up of gradual growth, are all visual experiences which we owe to the scientist, photographer and film maker. They have added enormously to our comprehension of the world, enabling us to

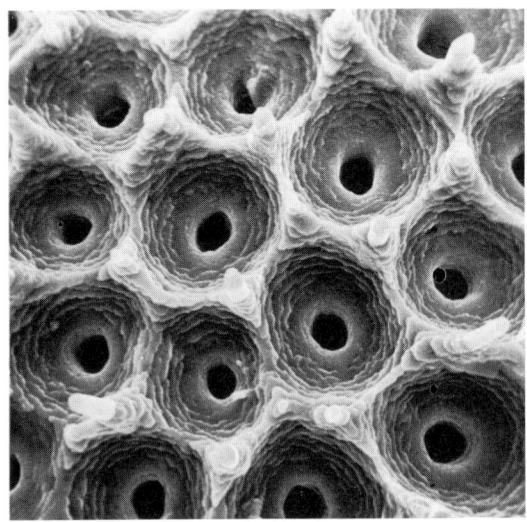

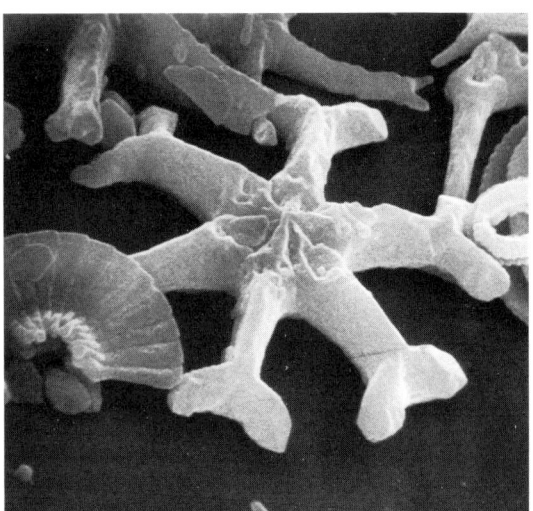

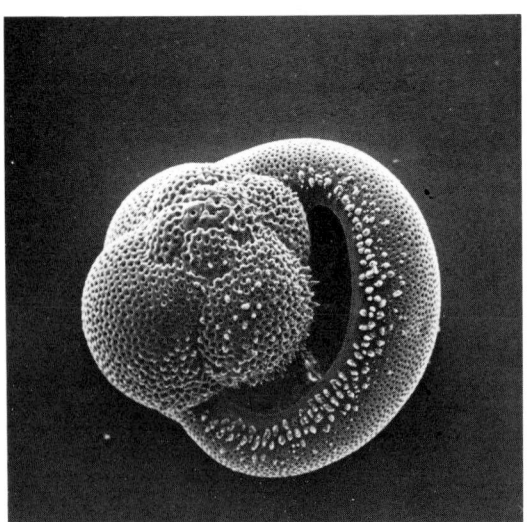

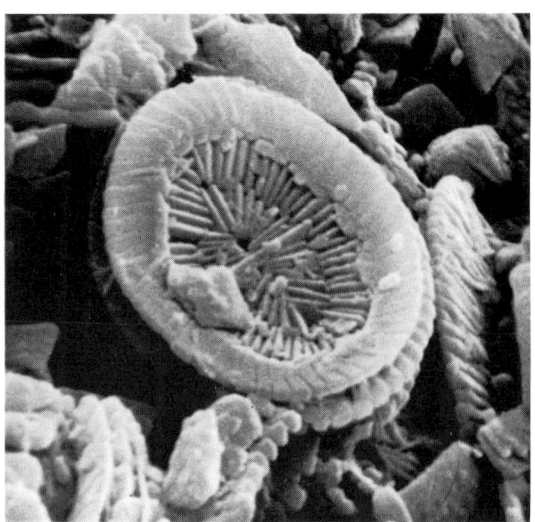

see it as a place in which an ordered pattern infuses the whole structure. It is this ordered rhythm which we try to understand and tap when we design anything based on natural forms.[1]*

When we really look closely at the natural world, what is often most intriguing is the subtle way in which a group of the 'same' things differ from each other. I mean by this the way in which, for example, no two leaves on a tree are ever the same as each other, no two twigs ever the same, no two stones, blades of grass, raindrops or ears of corn. Neither identical reproduction nor perfect symmetry

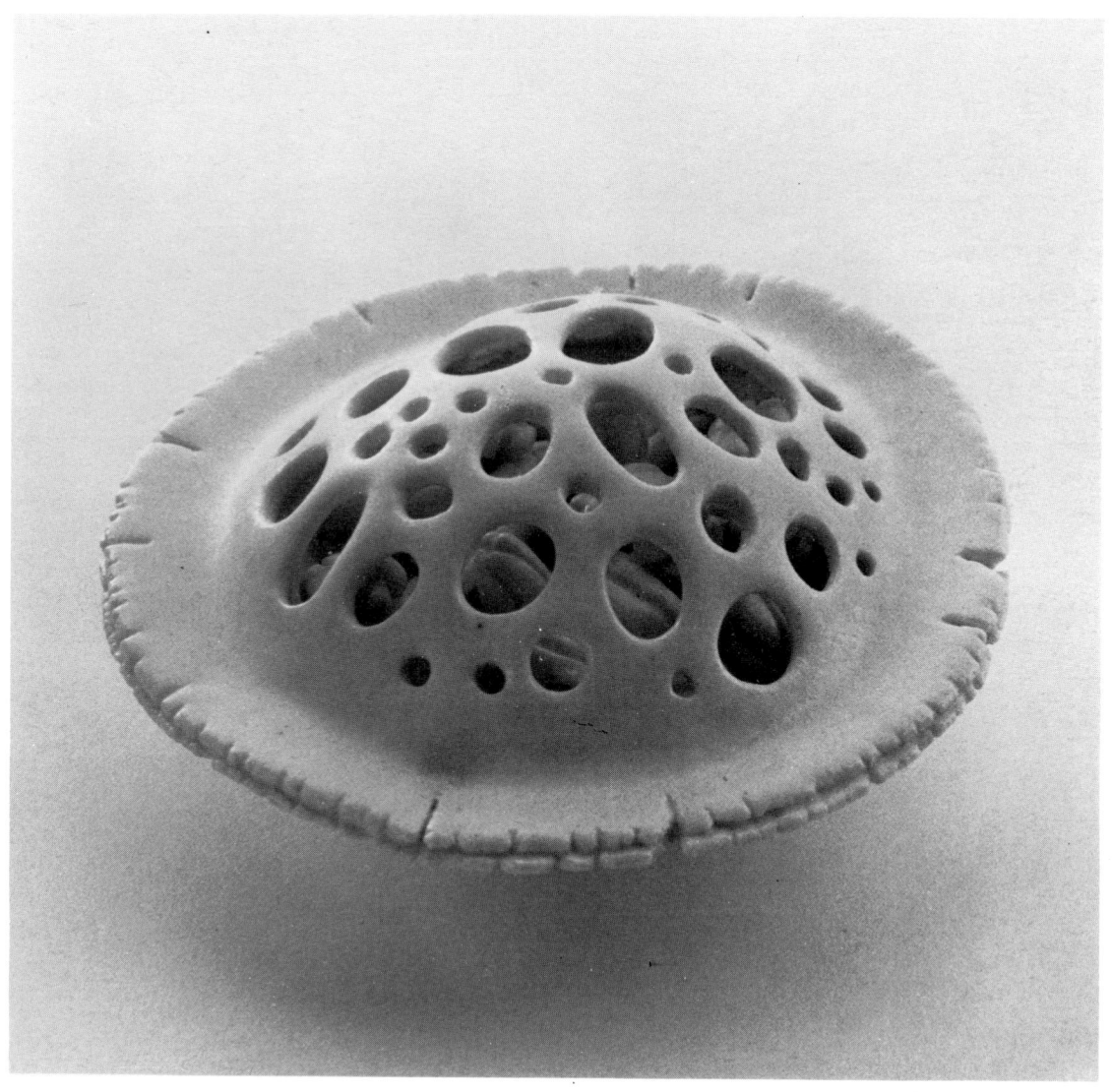

*The superior numbers which appear throughout the text, refer to a list of books on p. 148.

15

Silver birch leaves.

is found in nature, and it seems that it is this lack of 'perfect' symmetry that gives life to a thing, and makes it uniquely individual, so that it is itself and not able to be confused with any other. We get to know, recognize and love things because of their recognizable differences. We may respond to the massed effect of a number of factory-made identical objects, say a row of table-tennis balls, but after a while our eye begins to want to identify at least one separately. We are pleased to find, say, a speck or dent on one of them, then each time that we single it out we begin to feel a friendly recognition for it amongst the featureless and undifferentiated group of identical balls. If we understand the excitements of being a collector, in the broadest sense, we will

realize that the satisfaction is not in having as many identical things as possible, but as many similar things with slight differences; differences of shape, size and colour, which single out each thing from a group, and give it a separate identity. Even though they all recognizably belong to a 'family' of objects with the same name and 'family likeness' or group identity, one feature will be emphasized in one and diminished in another, however subtly, so giving variety and individuality.

Some of the richest images are those which conjure up more than one idea, hint at more than one starting point, making whole areas of disparate occurrences unify into one piece. In work in which visual ambiguity and analogy play a large part there is not usually just one

No two leaves, no two ears of corn, will ever be alike. A feature of design or form will be emphasized in one, diminished in another. There is no such thing as a 'perfect' leaf. The archetypal ear of corn is an average.

idea which prompted the making, but a collection of different starting points with a similar thread running through them all. The work will not then be a copy or translation of any existing form, but the creation of a new one which looks like a possible and convincing part of the natural world because it is designed with the same laws of growth, balance and movement that a natural form has.

I once read a Chinese saying that if a good pot were put down on a forest floor, a person should be able to walk by without noticing it, so well should it fit in and blend with its surroundings. That is a marvellous goal to try to attain for one kind of pottery. It does not mean, of course, that the pot should be totally negative and unremarkable. Quite the opposite, it means that it should be totally convincing in its unification with the natural materials and forms around it. Nothing in nature is negative or unremarkable after all.

Naturally the forest floor mentioned in the Chinese saying would only be the right setting in which to judge some types of pots, probably ash-glazed ones. Others would be more fairly judged by this method when put on a beach full of shells, and others in amongst a collection of semi-precious stones. These last two settings would naturally suit the crisper lines and clearer colours of porcelain.

Presumably this criterion would also work within the very different setting of twentieth-century city life, where pieces stemming from an imaginative response to the man-made environment would fit in with, say, the geometrically exact lines and pronounced colours of modern architecture, or the disembowelled innards and broken metalwork found in a graveyard for used cars.

These two areas of stimulation and interest, the city and the country, the urban and the natural, are not mutually exclusive. For example, the way that a poster peels off a wall, leaving patches adhering to its surface, can be as intriguing visually as layers of bark peeling off a tree. The growth of lichen on a surface may remind us of rust invading parts of a car.

An aerial view of the texture and pattern of streets and buildings can promote the same pattern-making urge as is sparked off by the complex structuring of leaf-ribs, or the branching out of river deltas.

In fact a very rich and often disturbing amalgam of references may be conjured up in one piece by hinting at both man-made mechanical forms and naturally occurring ones. This bringing together of images and the creation of visual metaphors is part of the stock-in-trade of the artist and designer. The idea need not be too specific, and strangely it may then communicate to the imagination more strongly than if it were.

But being excited about an idea and wanting to work it out in a chosen material does not always happen when we have the opportunity to get on with it straight away. Likewise when we do have the time and materials to hand the mind can be a blank.

I am sure that we all have our own mental amulets for use against imaginative sterility. For potters the necessary preparation of the clay by spiral wedging may be all that is needed to ease the senses into the right state of receptivity for spontaneous making. But when the mind still remains separate from the clay, and the flow of work does not start naturally, then I find it actually saves time to leave the workshop and the clay instead of fruitlessly messing about with it, and to refresh the imagination and sense of form by wandering about handling things and looking at the way in which they are formed—to consider such things as the way in which a leaf dries out, the similarities of articulation between animal joints and tree joints, between tree bark and human skin, between a feather and a leaf. No one can design in a vacuum; everything seen is stored away in the memory and everything made is a result of impressions received, conscious or not, of the known world, though they may be re-combined in fresh ways.

I have found myself that it is best not to try too hard to find any relevance to my work in what is being looked at. I may probably sketch things for their own sake, or to get their structure really clear in my mind, but not necessarily to think in terms of what I see and sketch being translated directly into clay. I find it best just to look analytically and constructively at whatever the eye picks out as being fascinating, and then whatever does catch the eye will automatically be found to be of relevance. The creative habit which we have built up by familiarizing ourselves with our materials then nudges us into activity. It is obvious that the more at home we are with our materials and techniques the easier and more spontaneous the process of creative interpretation should become.

In addition to this restocking of the vocabulary of forms, textures and colours by looking, handling and sketching, I have found another stimulus to the imagination when it is necessary to tune into work at short notice. This is to have a one-man brainstorming session. To do this give yourself a starting point. It may be the material itself which you intend to work with, or the germ of an idea which is struggling to get out. Select this central theme then let your mind run free and jot down in words or sketch-notes every association that comes to mind. Don't analyze or be critical at this stage, so as not to break the train of thought, just put it all down. From this seemingly undisciplined and unstructured rambling a pattern usually begins to emerge by itself. Actually it is not always easy to allow subconscious ideas to flow and link up without letting cerebral thinking take over. It demands a state of receptive concentration and passive activity—apparent contradictions on the surface—but it does work, and it throws up avenues for explorations which were there, in your mind, but hidden.

Avocado skins—all of these started more or less the same shape and size, in fact four of them were the matching halves of two complete fruits, yet all acquire different forms as they dry out.

LEFT *The dry skin from the end of a marrow. When the soft centre of the vegetable dries out, the skin tightens, folds and bends in on itself to a convoluted shape. The porcelain form* BELOW, *oxidized, 1300°C, is based on the dried marrow skin. 6 inches diameter, 1971*

The porcelain boxes RIGHT, *glazed in metallic black and fired to 1280°C, were based on an observation of the tightly packed and crumpled forms of petals inside flower buds, as exemplified by the poppy below. The boxes themselves open to reveal complex layers inside. 3½ and 2½ inches high, 1972.*

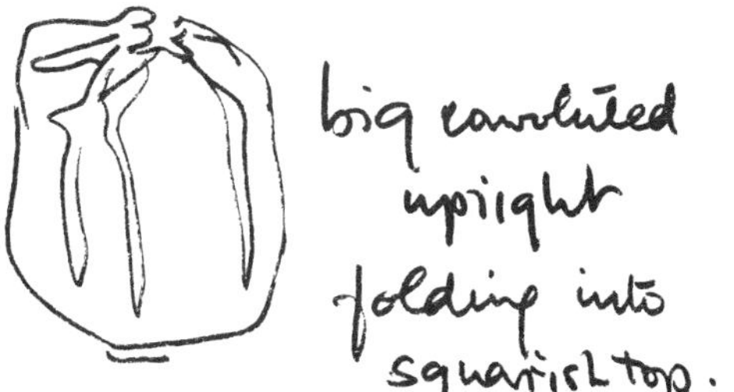

big convoluted
upright
folding into
squarish top.

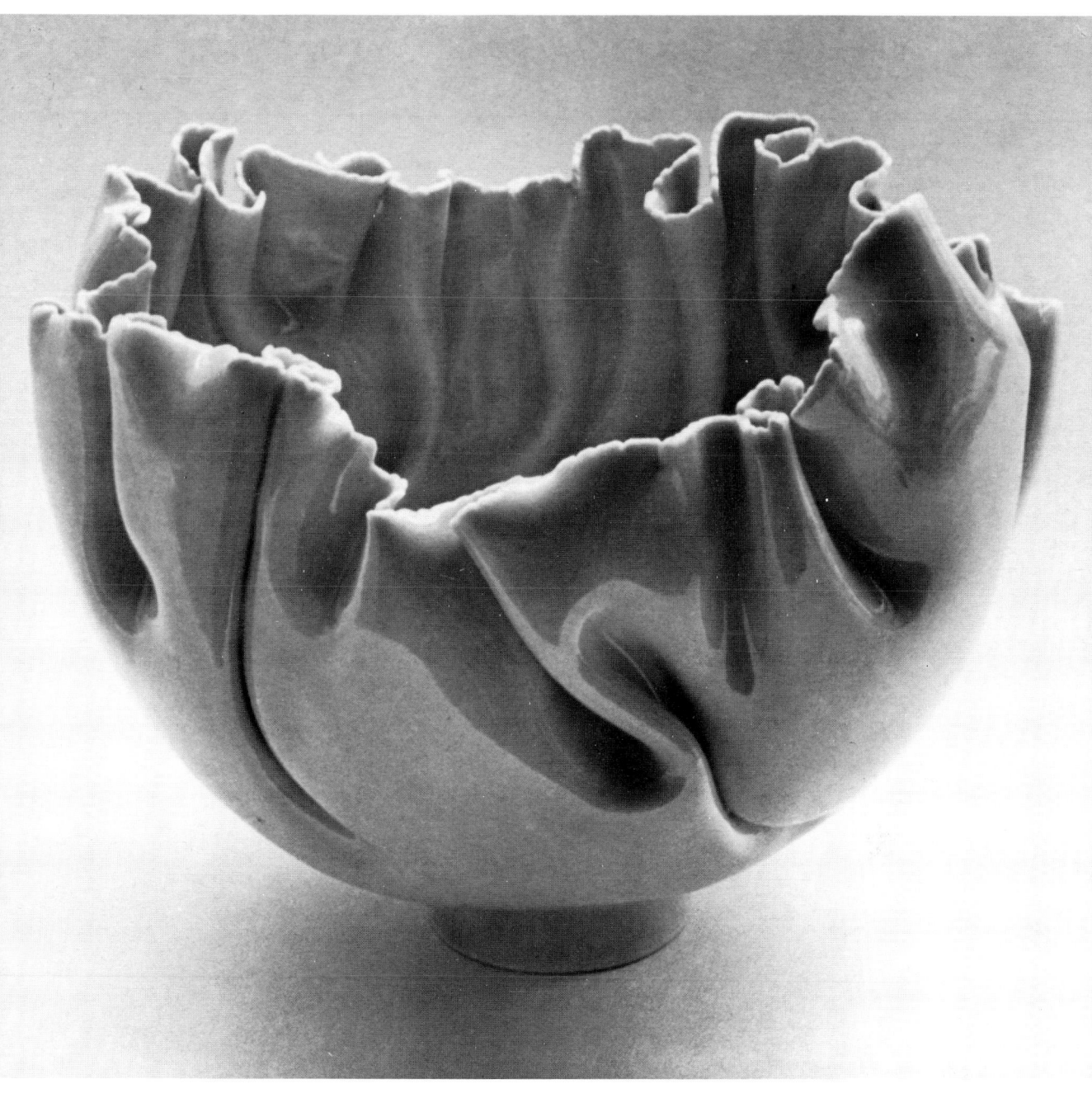

The pots ABOVE *and* LEFT, *oxidized, 1 300°C, are based on the forms of opening buds. The way in which fine petals overlap, creating areas of greater tonal density, is shown in the poppy* ABOVE LEFT *and recreated in the finely pinched walls of the opening flower form below it. Both pots approx. 5 inches diameter, 1975* LEFT, *1978* ABOVE.

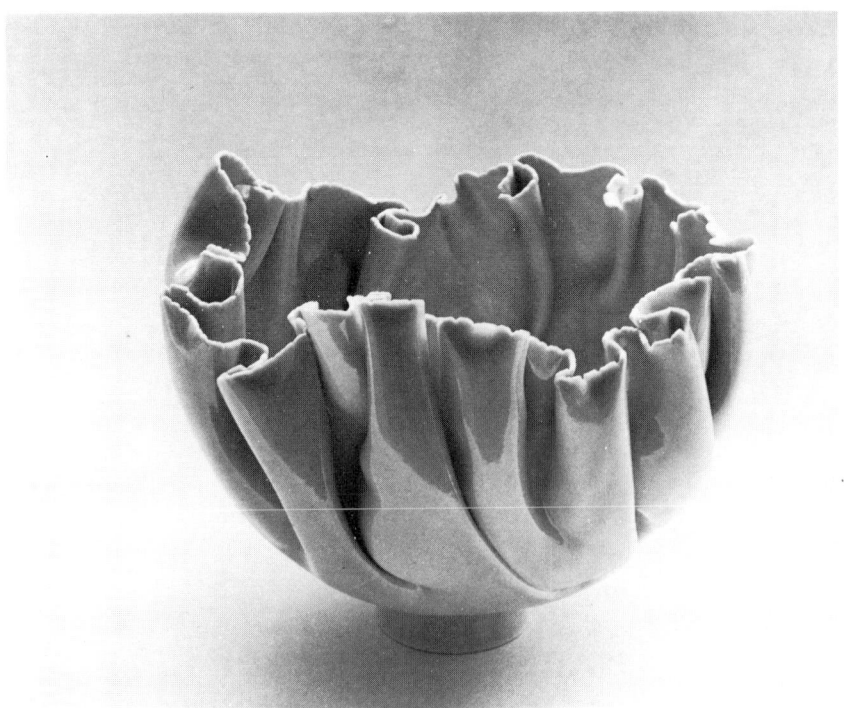

24

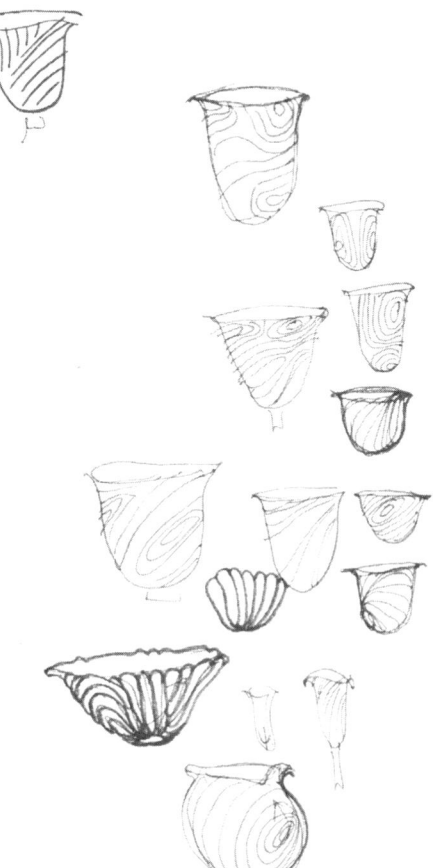

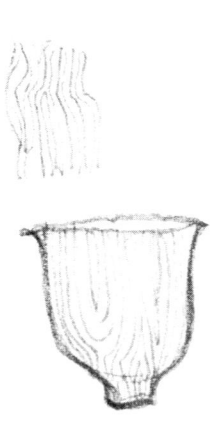

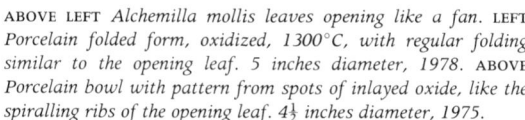

ABOVE LEFT *Alchemilla mollis leaves opening like a fan.* LEFT
*Porcelain folded form, oxidized, 1300°C, with regular folding
similar to the opening leaf. 5 inches diameter, 1978.* ABOVE
*Porcelain bowl with pattern from spots of inlayed oxide, like the
spiralling ribs of the opening leaf. 4½ inches diameter, 1975.*

25

The fully open, gently undulating leaf of Alchemilla mollis.

ABOVE *and* RIGHT *Veined leaf forms in porcelain, oxidized, 1300°C. The veining was painted on with oxides under the glaze. The upright form was made from two shallow pinched bowl forms which were joined at their edges with slurry, and balanced on a small pinched-out foot, also joined on with slurry.* ABOVE *7 inches diameter, 1975,* RIGHT *4 inches high, 1975.*

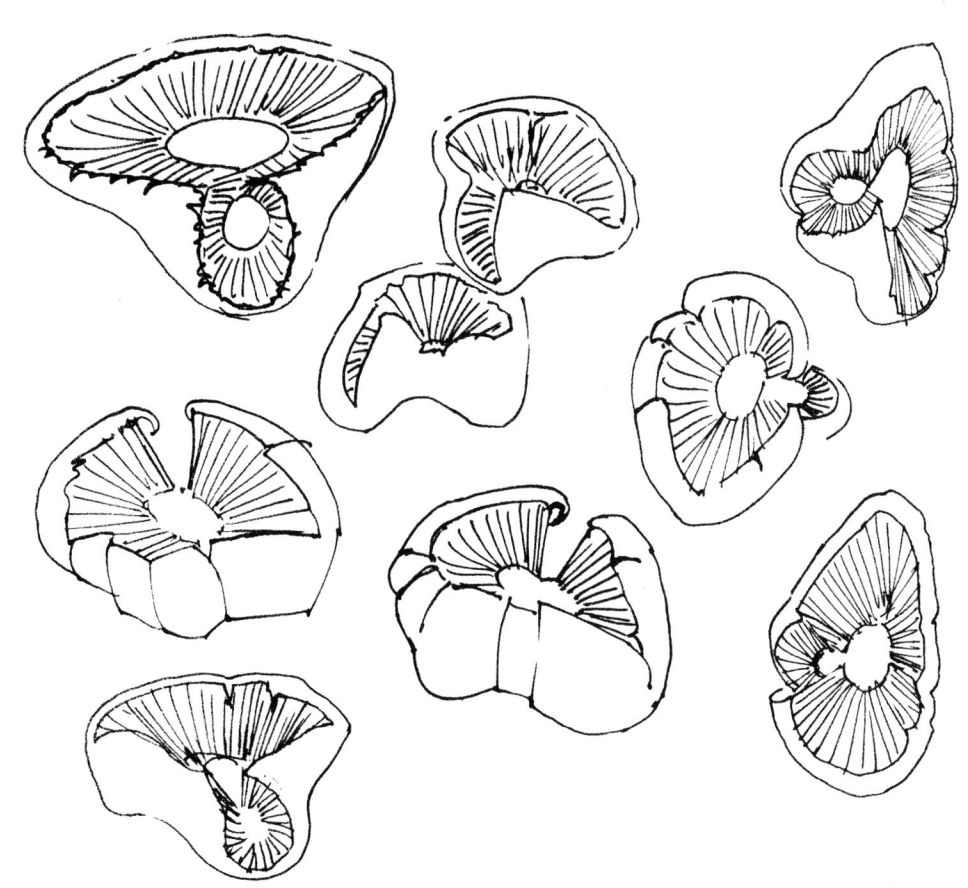

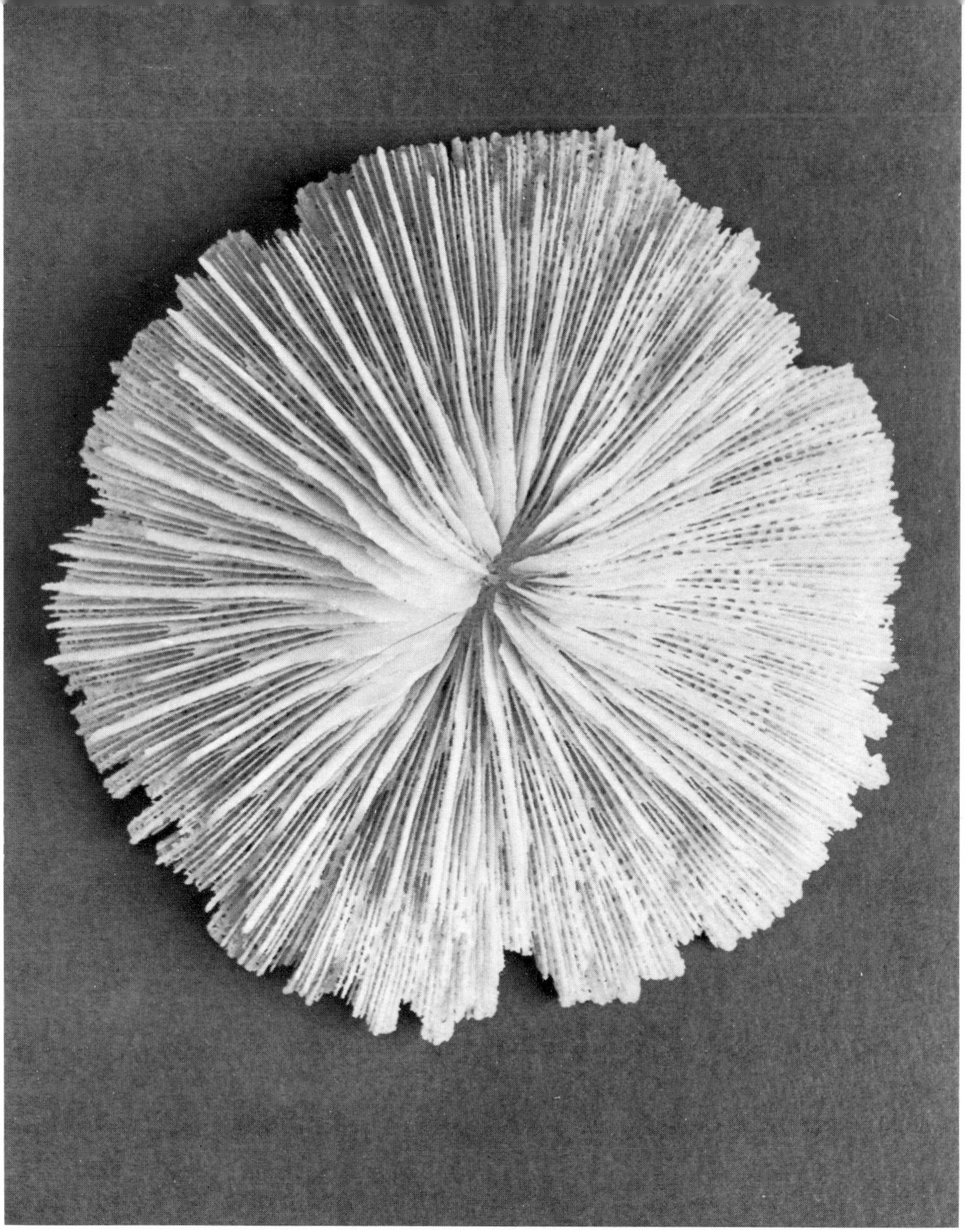

ABOVE *Mushroom coral.* FAR RIGHT *Porcelain coral form, oxidized, 1300°C, ash glaze, 4½inches diameter, 1973. Variations of translucency are achieved by the carving, contrasting the raised ridges with the thinner carved-out grooves.*

Surface of Indian ocean coral

30

'Carved Veined Leaf Form'. Porcelain, oxidized, 1300°C, made from three separate pinched forms joined together. The veining was carved into the dry porcelain before glazing. 3 inches high.

Coral ridginging round into centre.

LEFT 'Shadow Form'. The coloured areas correspond to the actual shadows cast over the main body by the raised parts. 5 inches diameter, 1976.

Water Rippling
and swirling

light through trees
dappling on ground.

The immense variety of patterning on such creatures as zebra, deer LEFT, fish, moths FAR LEFT and beetles has evolved for practical purposes, so that the animals may blend into their environment. The pots illustrated are decorated with camouflage patterns. The interlocking designs wander from the inside to the outside of the forms joining across the exterior and interior surfaces, and so losing the natural divisions of the form in the way that the true shapes of many living creatures are confused by camouflage coloration. Bowl TOP $3\frac{3}{4}$ inches diameter, 1976, ABOVE and LEFT 5 inches, 1975.

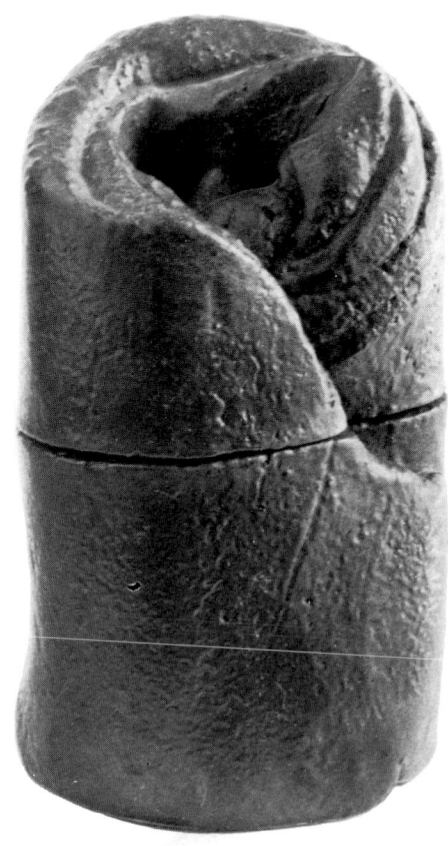

Sometimes forms and patterns are suggested by the shapes which the clay itself takes on at various stages whilst it is being formed. Spiral wedging produces rhythmic shapes which may be used as a basis. A spirally-wedged piece of clay was slightly flattened on its base and sides, and then made into a box RIGHT by cutting off the top, and hollowing out the interior with a wire tool. Stoneware, metallic black glaze, oxidized, 1280°C, 4½ inches high, 1969.

The overlapping folds of spiral wedging suggested the hilly landscapes BELOW. These were carved out to give 'caves' (thus forming a wall of an even thickness), and clumps of modelled trees were added to the summits to add further to the illusion. Porcelain, oxidized, 1300°C, 3 inches long, 3 inches high, 1972.

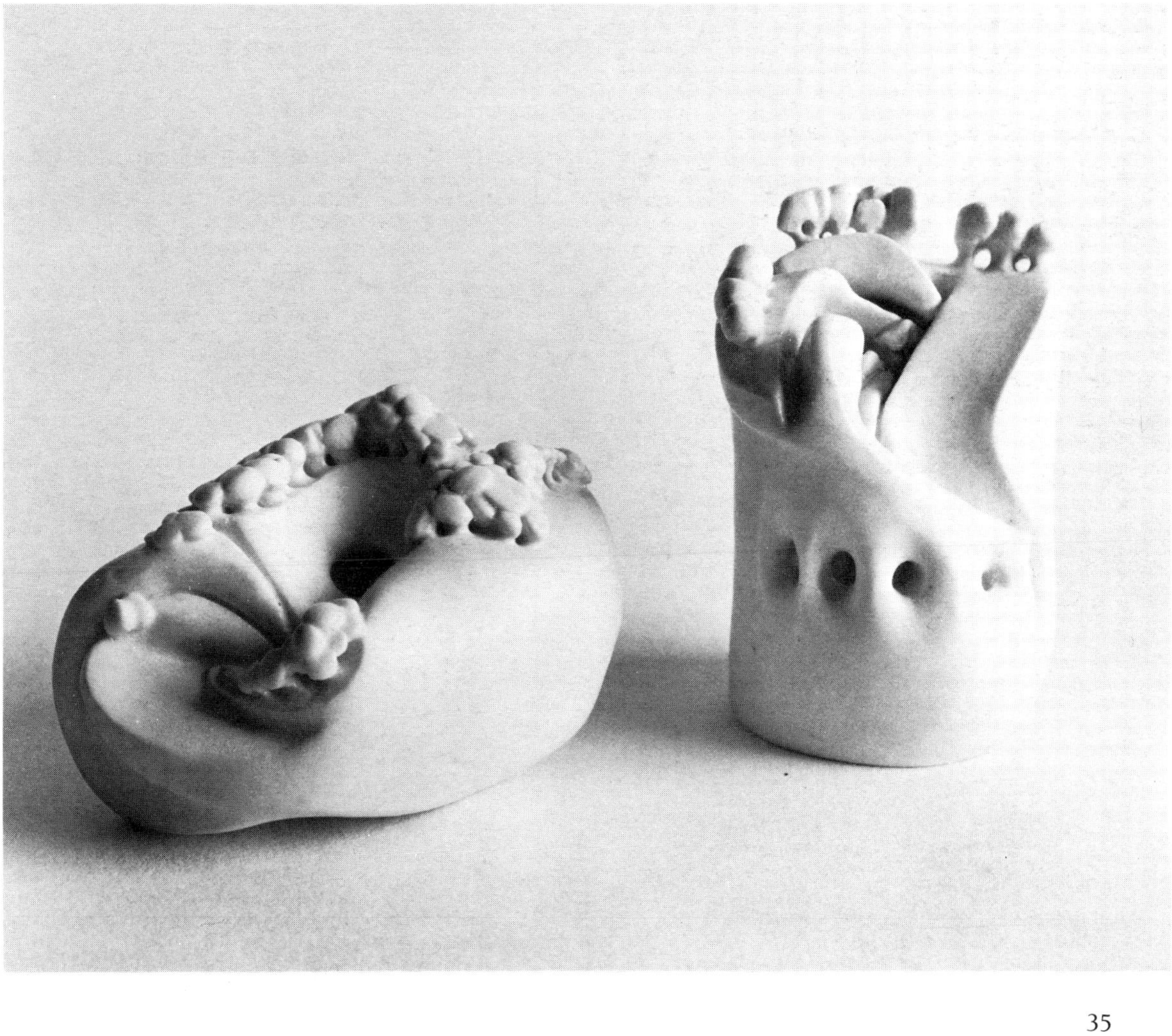

'Split-edged Bowl'. Stoneware, oxidized, 1280°C. The pinching out
of this bowl was purposely carried out past the plastic stage of the
clay, so that the sides split and bent, as many natural forms do as
they dry out. 7 inches wide, 1968.

36

'Split-edged Bowl with Dappled Interior'. Porcelain, oxidized, 1300°C, 5 inches wide, 1975. The main bowl form was pinched whilst the clay was still plastic, but the top edge was pinched when the clay was drying out to split and curl like the dried flower head LEFT.

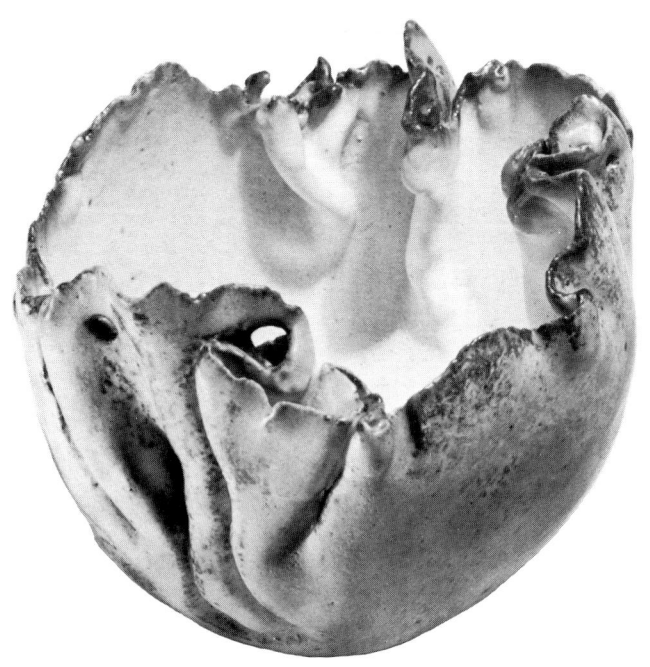

Forms made in stoneware have very different qualities from those made in porcelain, even when handled in exactly the same way. In the convoluted form LEFT the clay has a static earthbound look. The outside has a coating of slip under the glaze. Stoneware, oxidized, 1280°C, 8 inches wide, 1968. The fluidity and lightness of the porcelain convoluted bowl RIGHT make it seem to float, in direct contrast to the heavy look of stoneware. Oxidized, 1300°C, 7 inches diameter, 1974. Even in a closed form, porcelain has a light quality. 'White Wave' BELOW was made of two 'skins'—an outer pinch-built bowl, with the inner 'waves' separately formed and eased into position. Porcelain, oxidized, 1300°C, 6 inches diameter, 1974. Collection, Museum of Modern Art, New York.

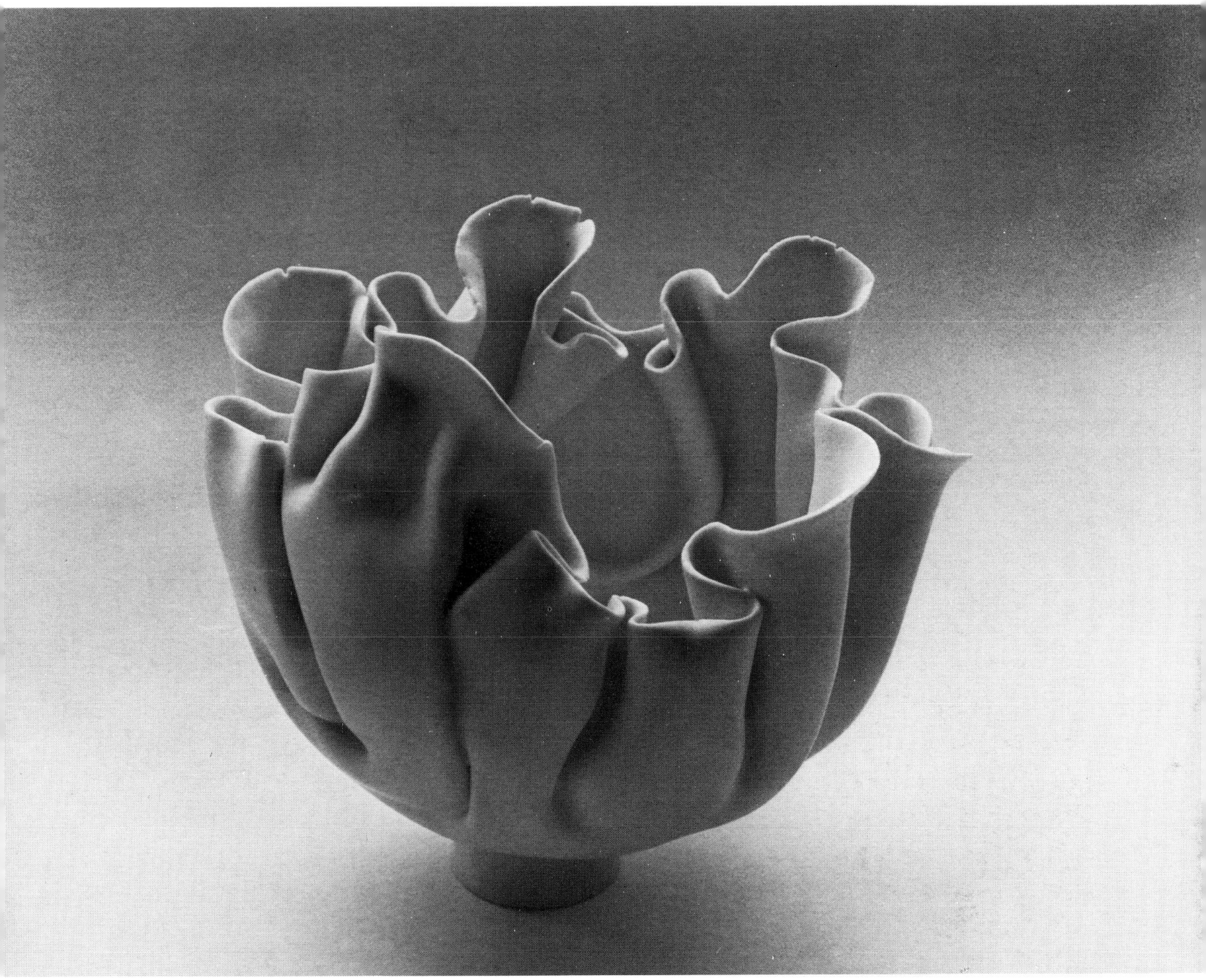

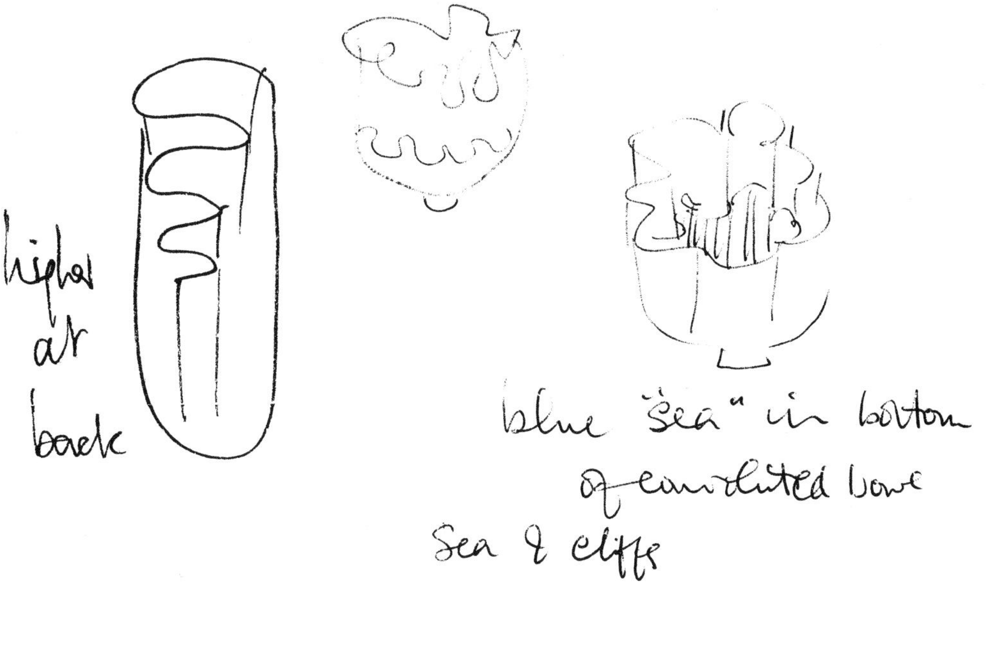

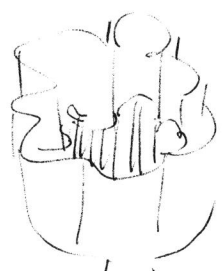

at
back

blue "sea" in bottom
of convoluted bowl

Sea & cliff

BELOW *The stoneware form is similar to 'White Wave' on page 38, and is made in the same way, but it has a weightier appearance, partly because of the stoneware material of which it is made. Oxidized, 1280°C, 7 inches wide, 1973.*

RIGHT *'Stoneware Bowl'. Coiled and pinched, 1280°C. The natural unevenness of the rim has the solid look of a line of mountains,* enhanced by stopping the coating of slip short of the top edge, so that it is white-tipped with the white glaze. 7 inches wide, 1973. BELOW RIGHT *Porcelain bowl. White glazed, oxidized, 1300°C. The natural unevenness of the rim in this case was carved to give the appearance of a tree-edged hill, enhancing the light-catching qualities of the translucent porcelain. 5 inches diameter, 1976.*

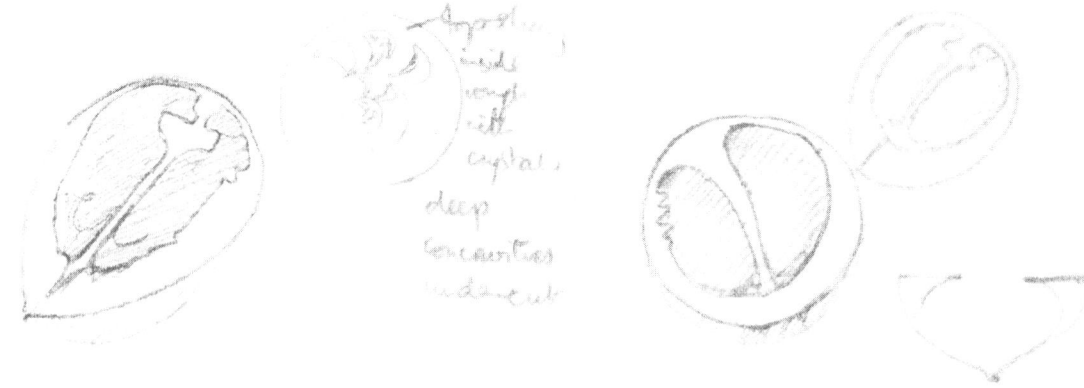

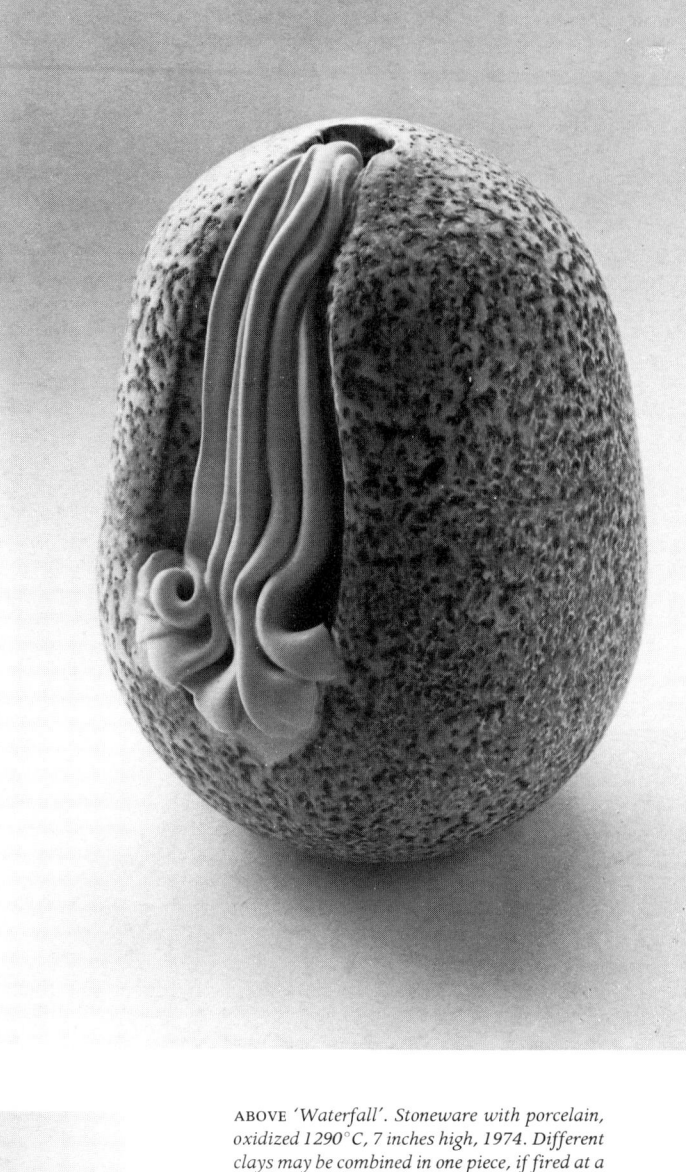

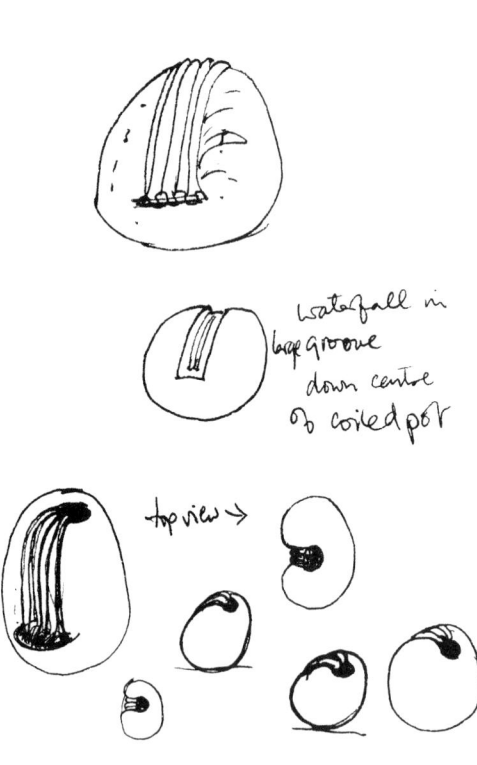

waterfall in
large groove
down centre
of coiled pot

top view →

ABOVE 'Waterfall'. Stoneware with porcelain, oxidized 1290°C, 7 inches high, 1974. Different clays may be combined in one piece, if fired at a suitable temperature for both. The different qualities of each may be emphasized by their combination, also shown in 'Spring' LEFT, stoneware with porcelain, oxidized, 1290°C, $4\frac{3}{4}$ inches wide, 1974. In each case the boulder form was coiled in stoneware clay, and the 'water' was pinched out of porcelain.

On the facing page is a piece of agate, with varying translucency according to the mineral content. The same effect is achieved in the 'Sliced Stone' bowl BELOW, in which uncoloured 'windows' allow light clearly to pass through the porcelain wall, and coloured parts reduce translucency, as in semi-precious stones. $6\frac{1}{4}$ inches wide, 1977.

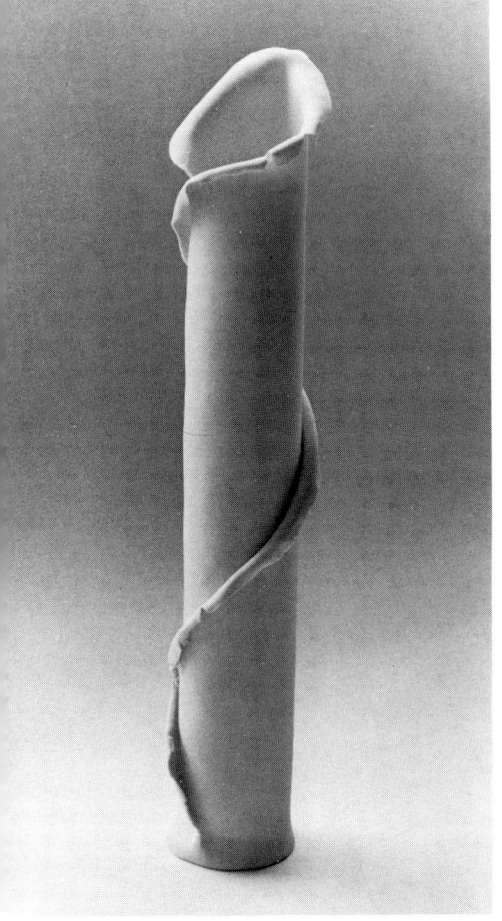

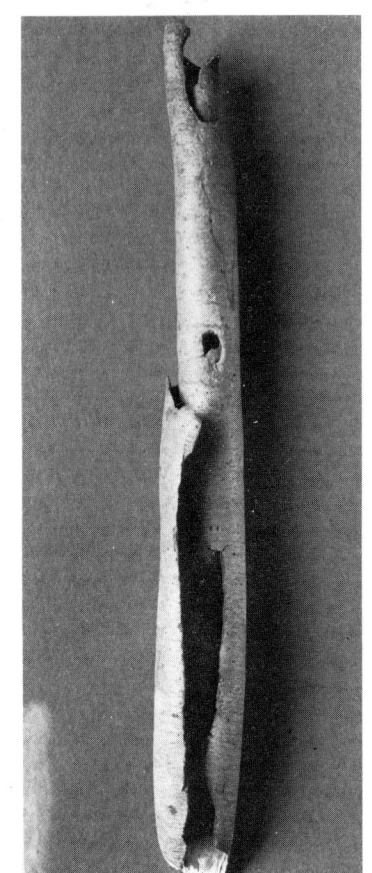

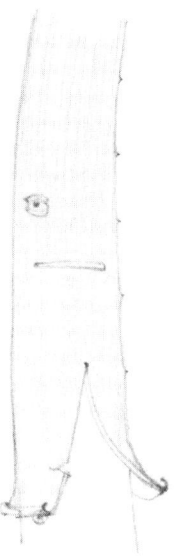

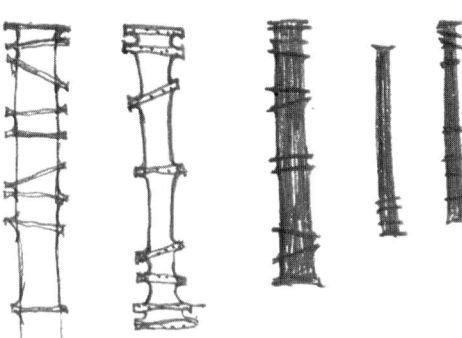

44

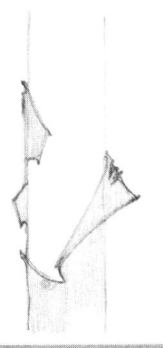

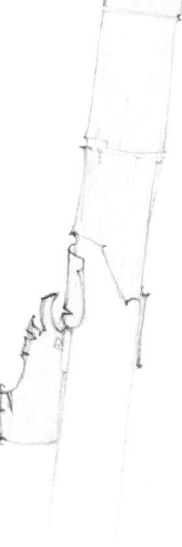

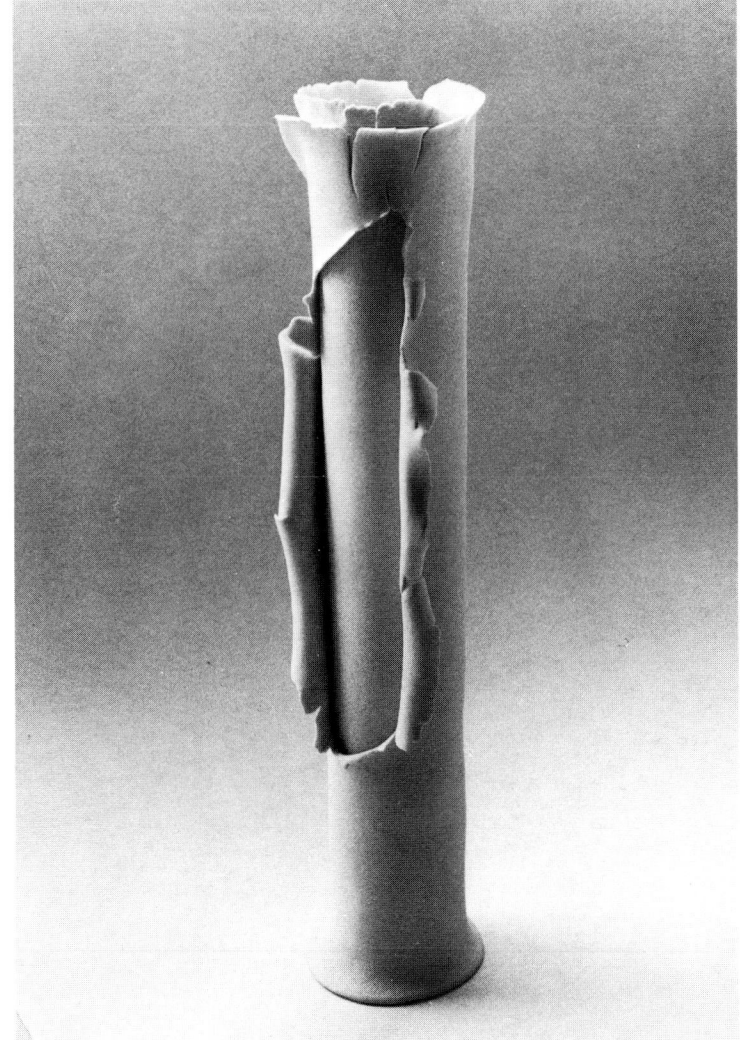

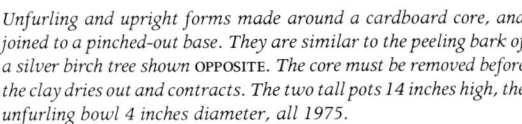

Unfurling and upright forms made around a cardboard core, and joined to a pinched-out base. They are similar to the peeling bark of a silver birch tree shown OPPOSITE. *The core must be removed before the clay dries out and contracts. The two tall pots 14 inches high, the unfurling bowl 4 inches diameter, all 1975.*

whole surface
made up of
overlapping
square
slabs

45

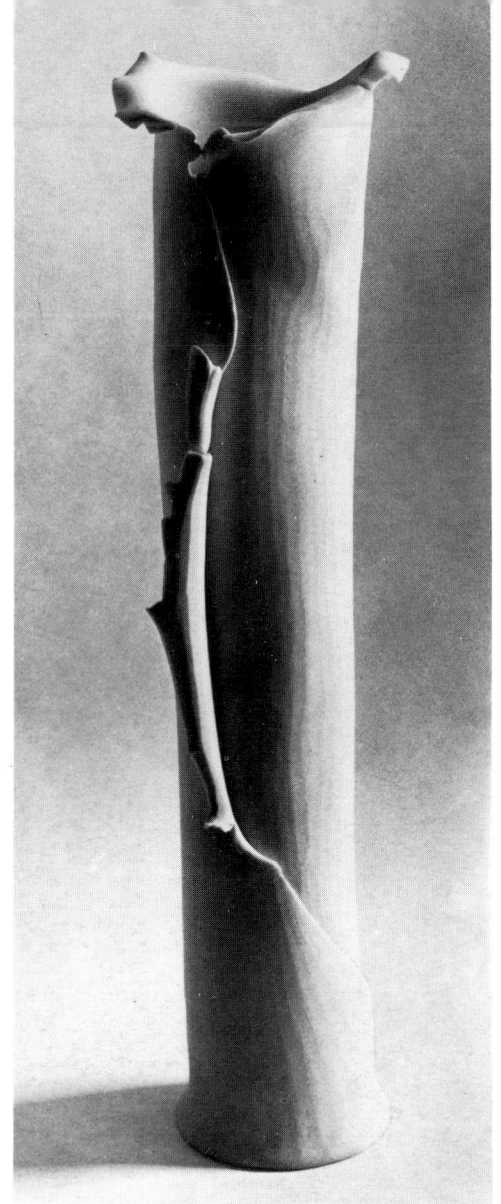

Standing forms based on growing plants. The wrapped and joined cylinders of porcelain BELOW *and* FAR RIGHT *have had the top sections pinched out finely so that they widen and spread like a flower.* LEFT *14 inches high, 1975,* BELOW *8 inches high, 1974;* LOWER RIGHT *9 and 6 inches high, 1966,* FAR RIGHT *9 inches high, 1973.*

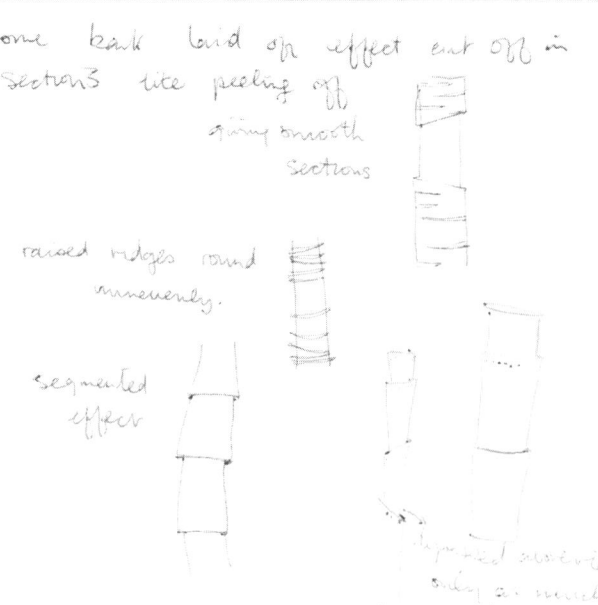

Some bark laid on effect cut off in
sections like peeling off
giving smooth
sections

raised ridges round
unevenly.

segmented
effect

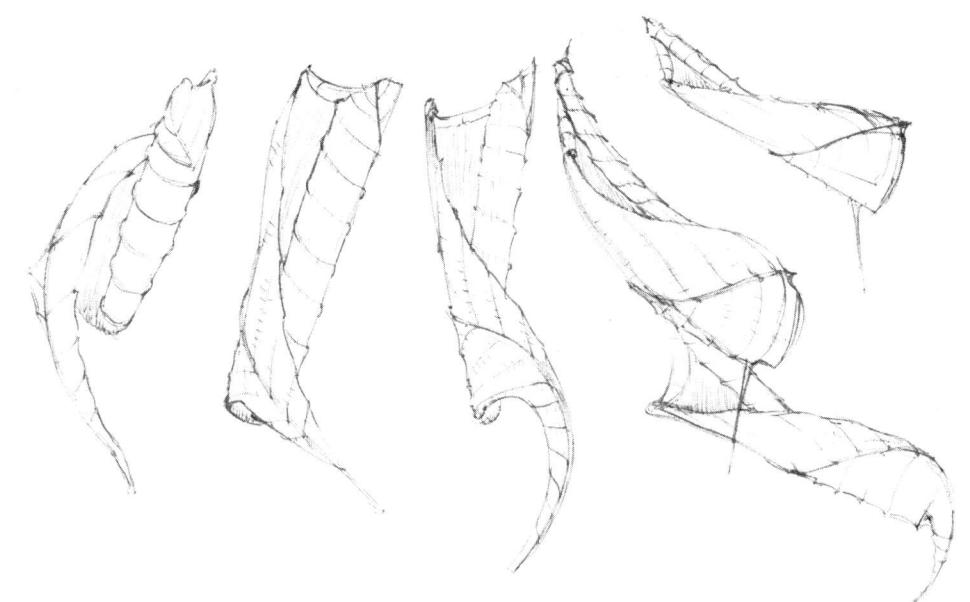

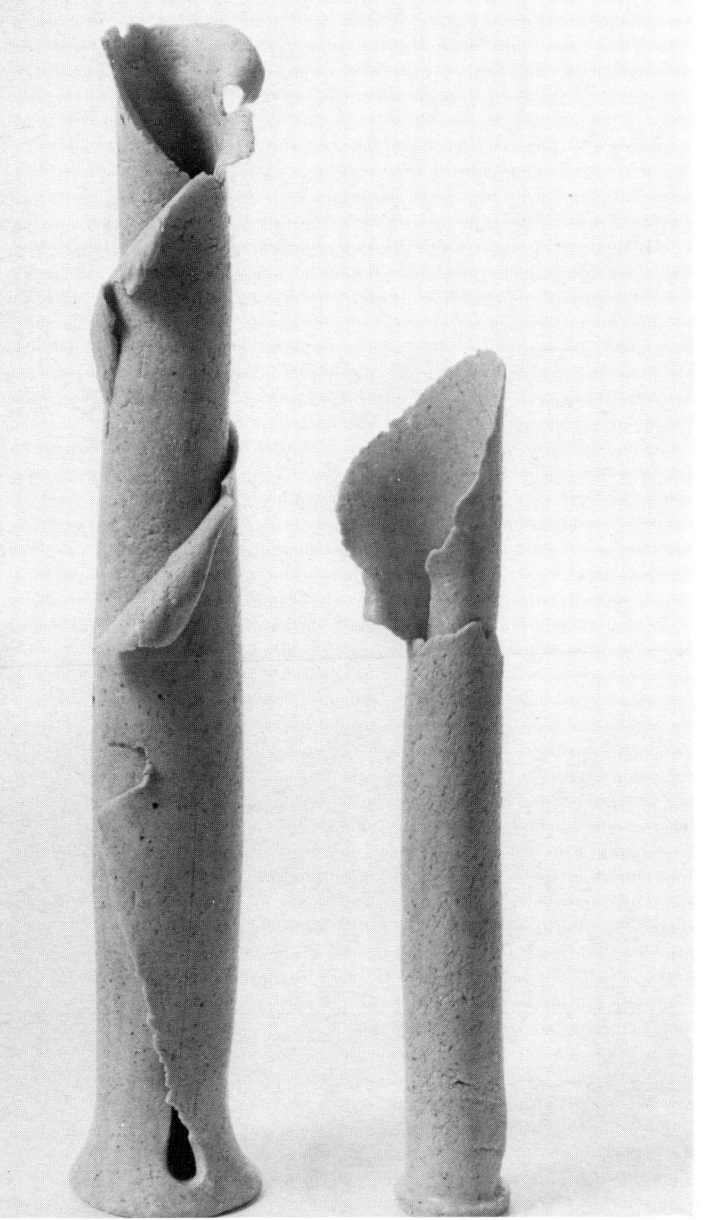

47

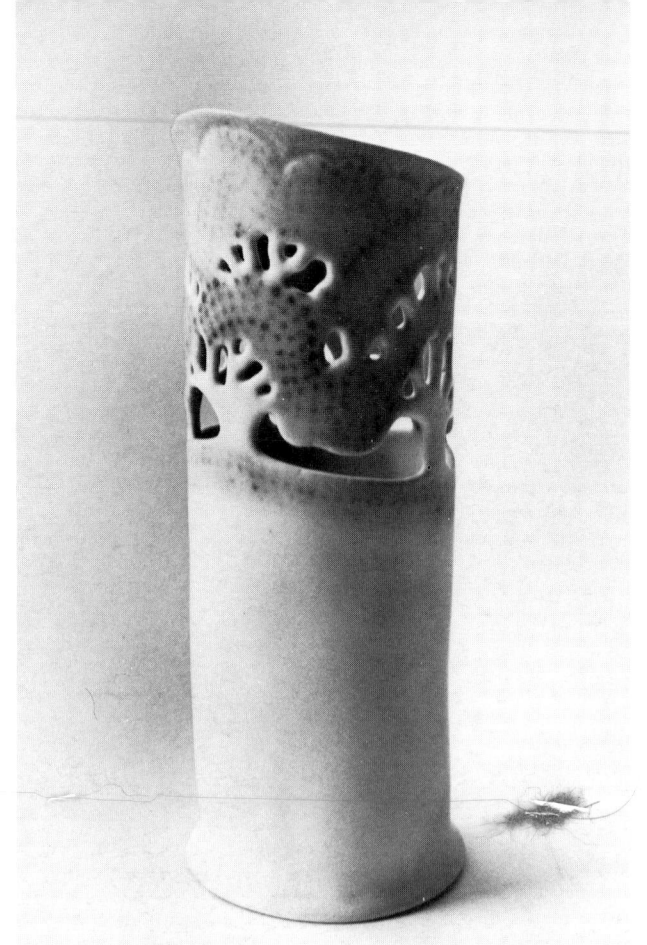

There are many ways of interpreting features of landscape in clay. In the 'Landscape-edged Canyon' BELOW and the 'Tree-edged Dry Valley' RIGHT I have used the naturally undulating and uneven rims of the pinched bowls to suggest a line of hills with the silhouette broken by clumps of trees. In the 'Tree-edged Column' LEFT the carved patterns of the trunks and branches of the trees themselves carry the emphasis. 7 inches high, 1974. BELOW 6 inches wide, 1974, RIGHT 5 inches diameter, 1977.

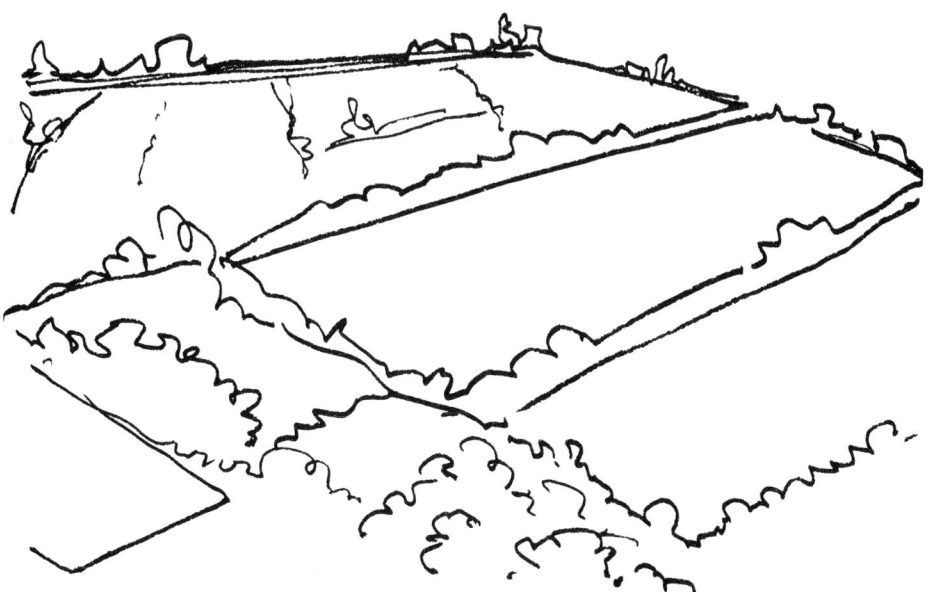

Allegorical landscapes in porcelain. LEFT *'Tree Apple'*, 3¾ inches wide, 1977; LEFT, BELOW *'Symbolic Landscape'*, 5½ inches wide, 1977, BELOW *'River Birth'*, 7 inches diameter, 1976.

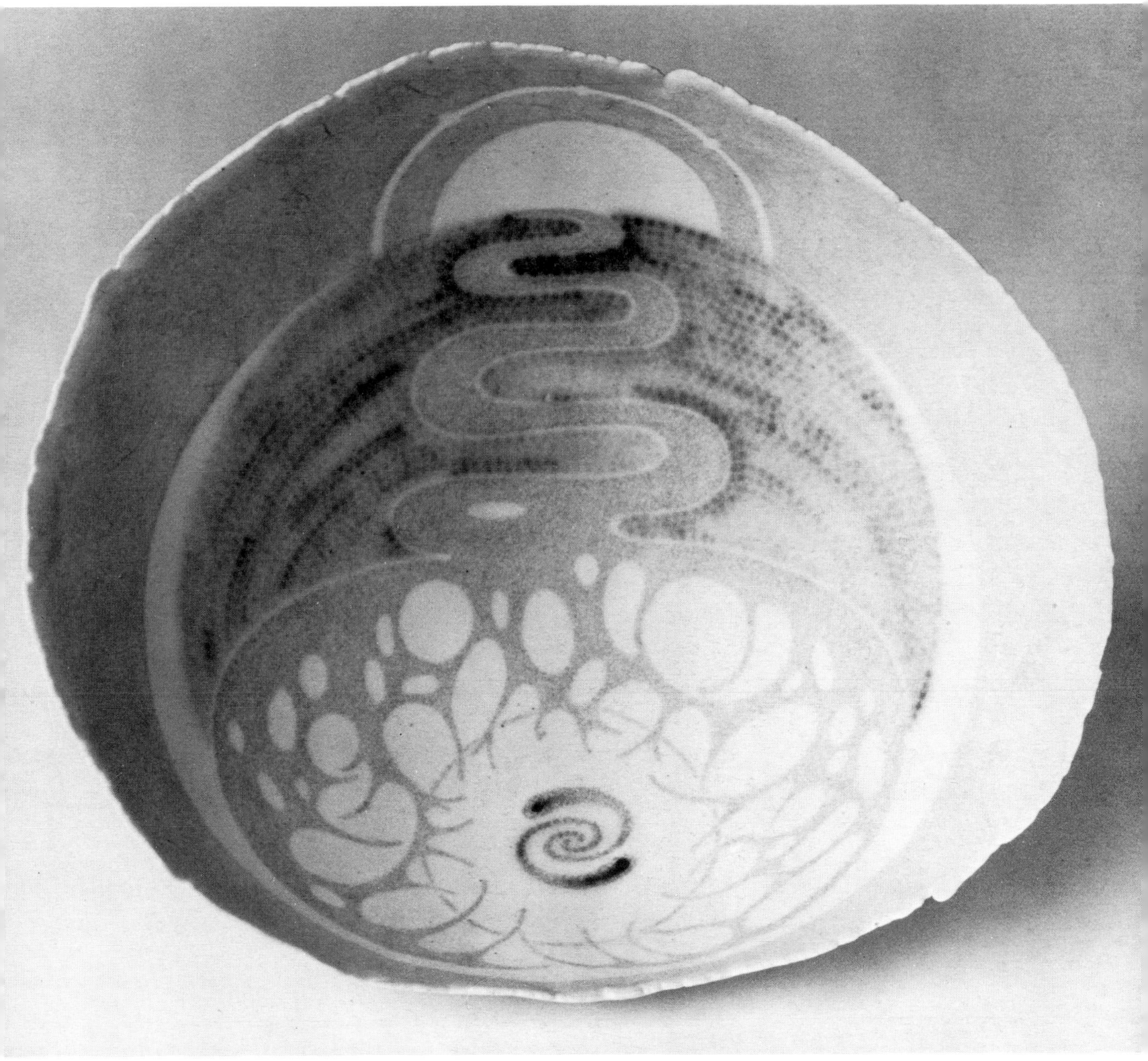

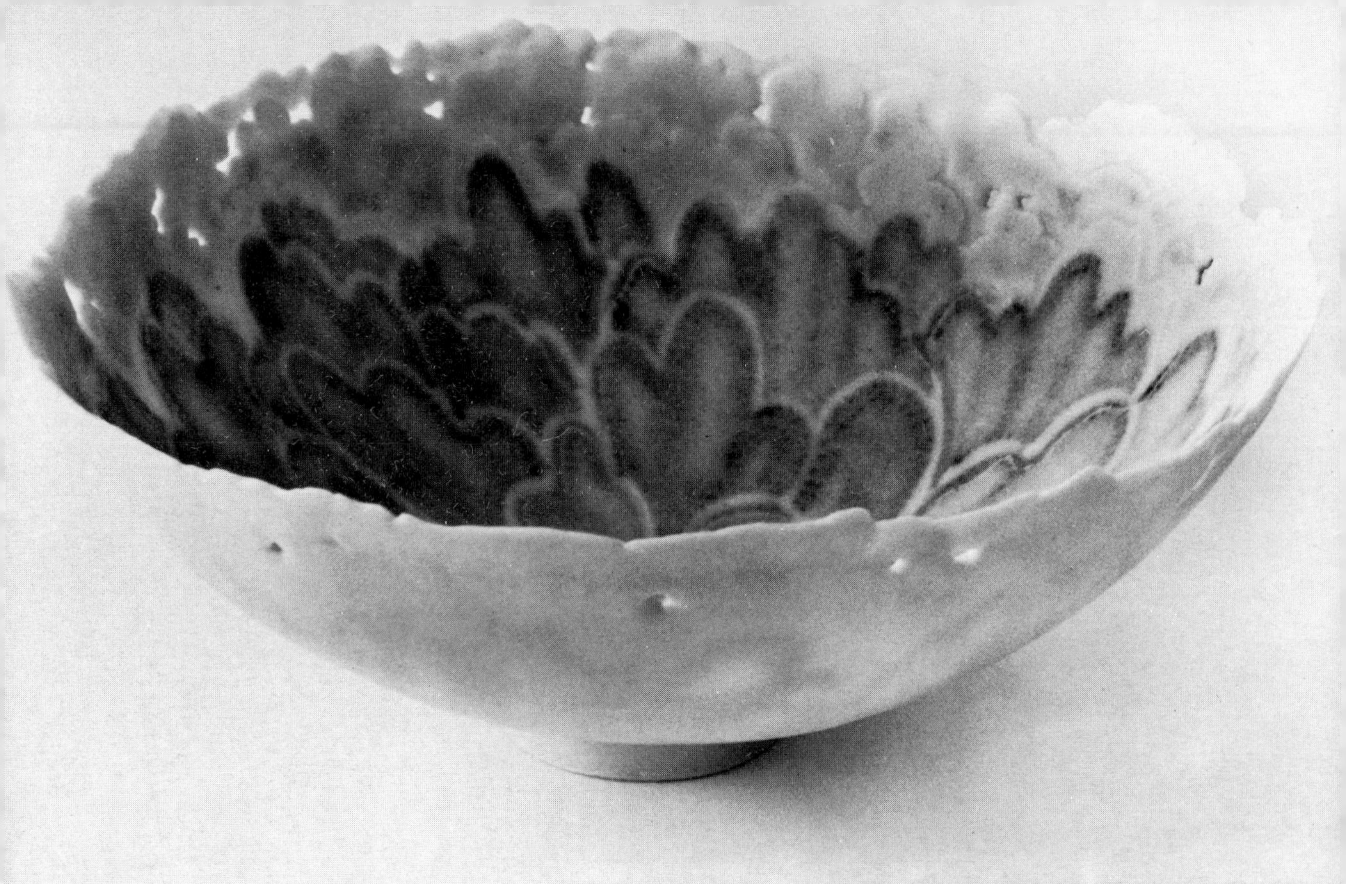

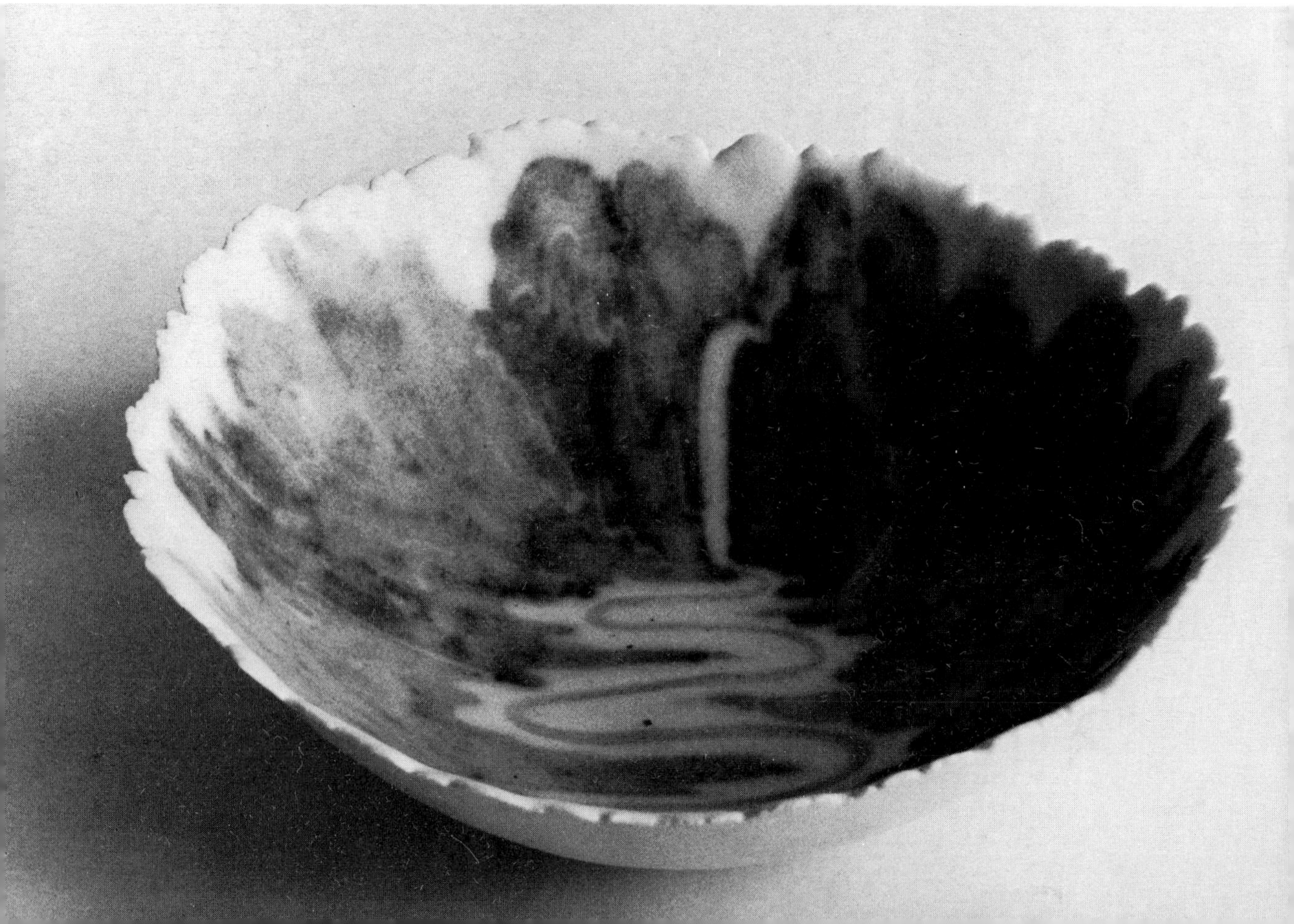

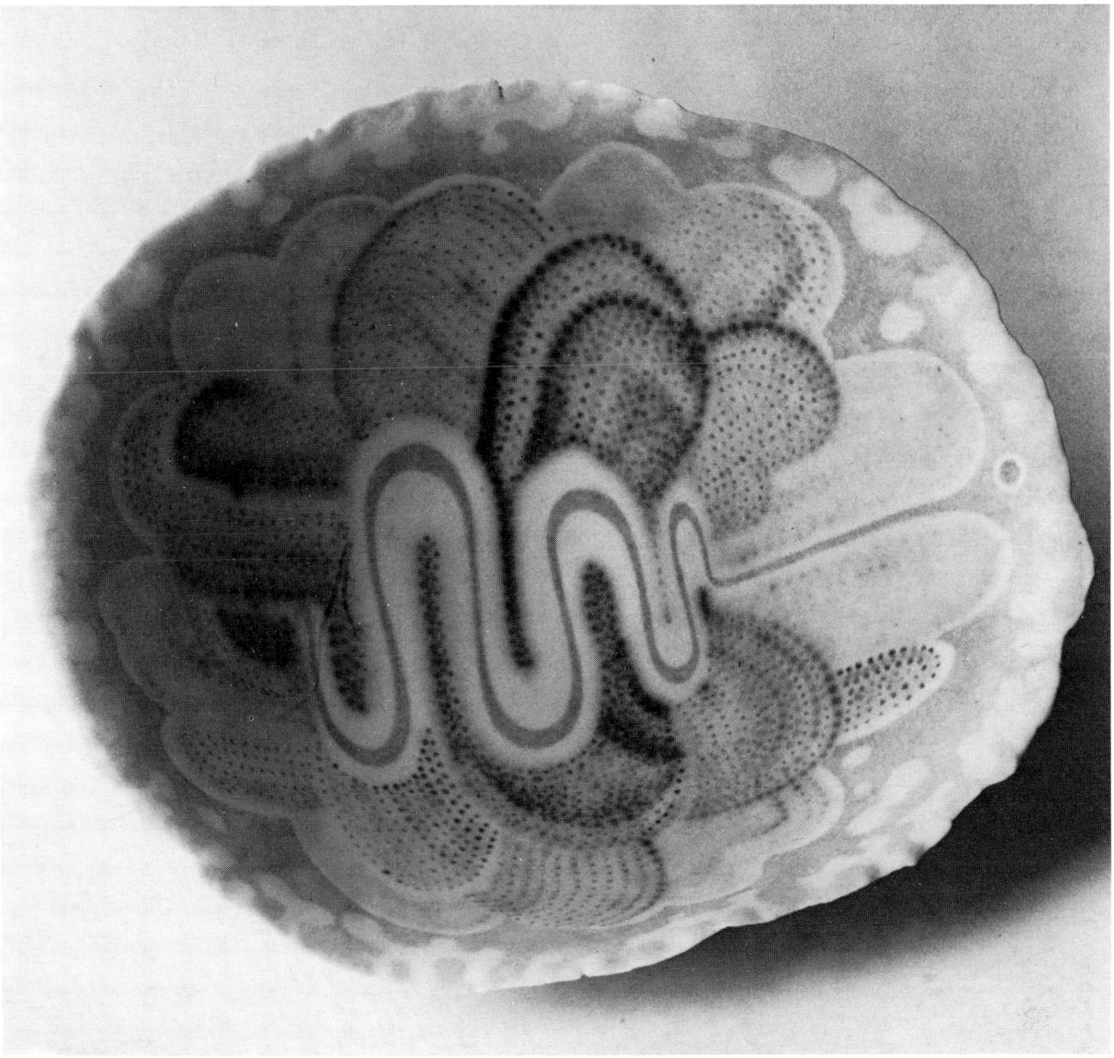

Large plate
+ raised waves
+ painting
paint ridges
on folds.

TOP LEFT *'Blue Hills with Carved Edge', $6\frac{1}{2}$ inches diameter, 1975.*
LOWER LEFT *'Enclosed Valley', 6 inches diameter, 1975.* ABOVE
'River Valley', 7 inches diameter, 1975.

53

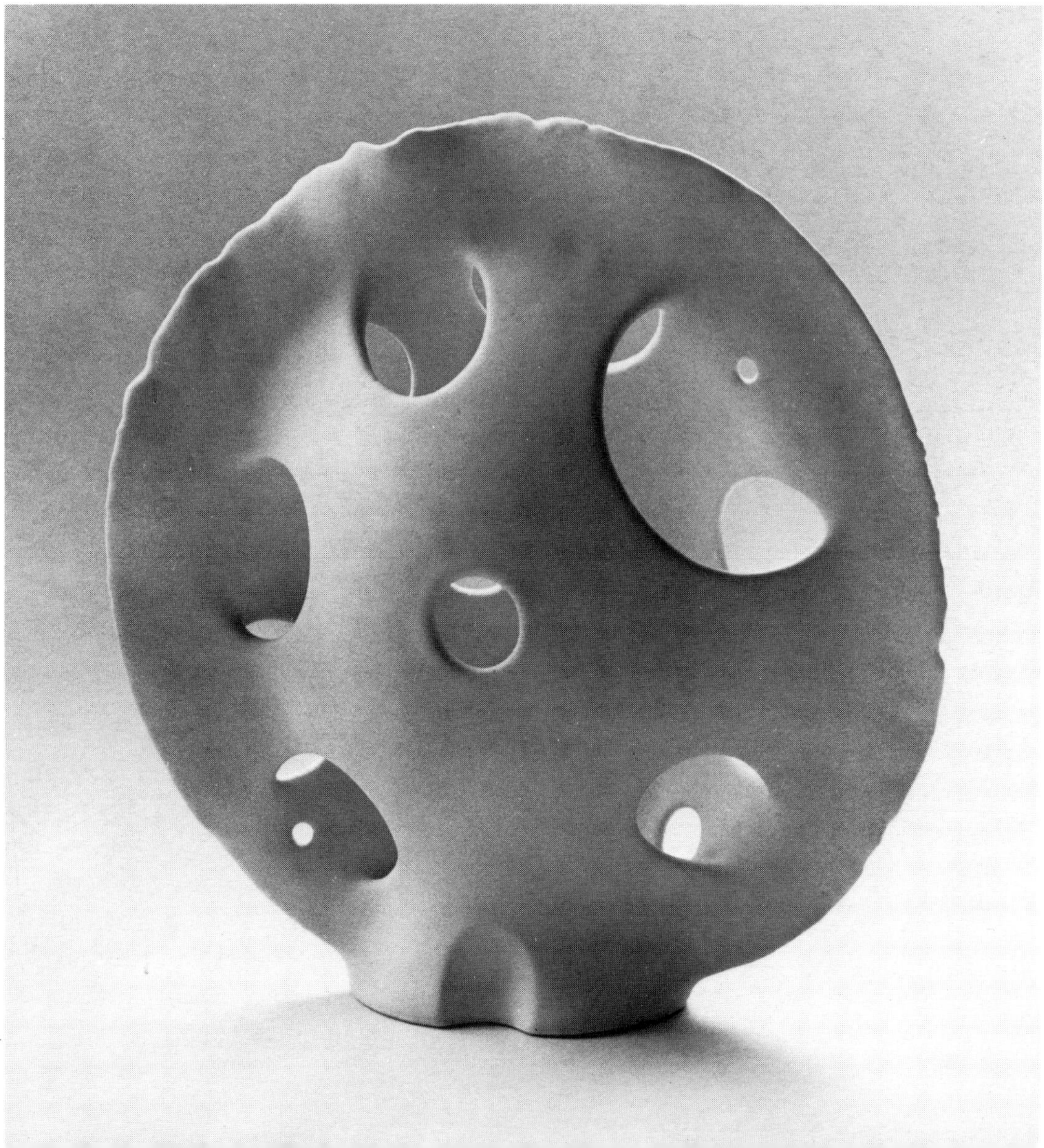

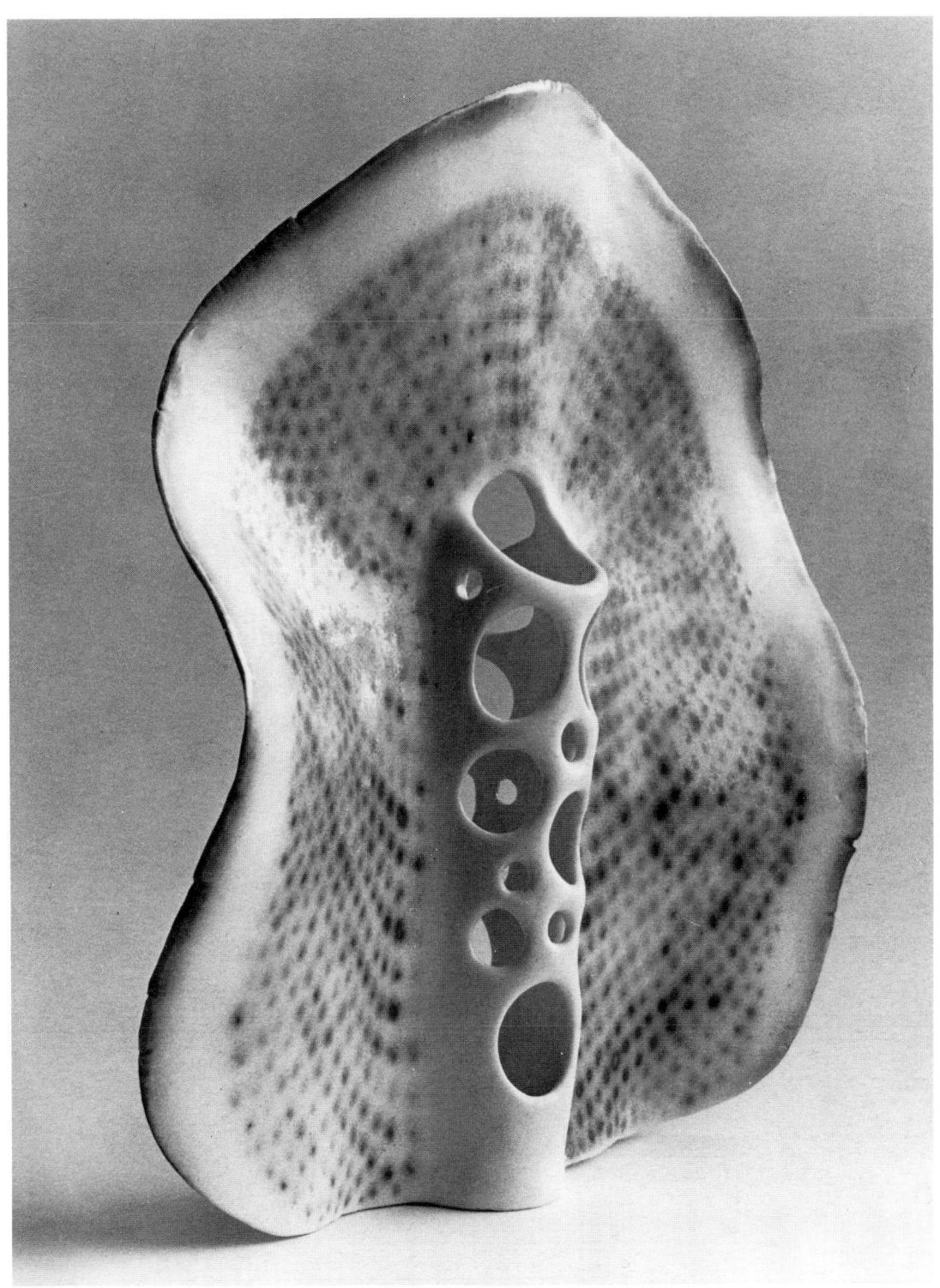

Shown here and on the next two pages are examples of double or treble forms. The pieces are built up out of separately pinched-out bowls and sheets, which are joined together in exactly the same way as the footring is joined to a pot. Made between 1972 and 1975, they range from 4½ inches diameter to 7 inches high.

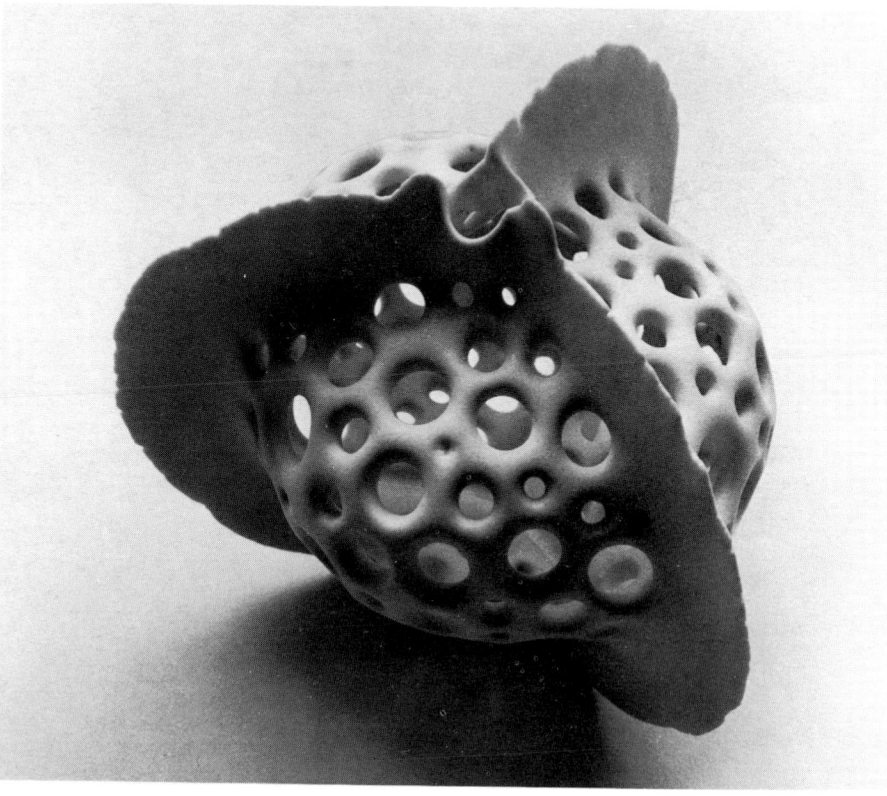

BELOW *Three separately pinched pieces of porcelain, each shaped like a segment of orange peel, were joined along their edges. These were then pinched to form ribs encircling a sphere, which was then pierced. 3½ inches diameter, 1974. Collection of Musée des Arts Decoratifs, Lausanne.*

Lidded pots. The pot on the left has a deeply carved design on both body and lid. 6 inches high, 1968. In the pots below, only the lids are carved and pierced. 3 inches diameter, 1966.

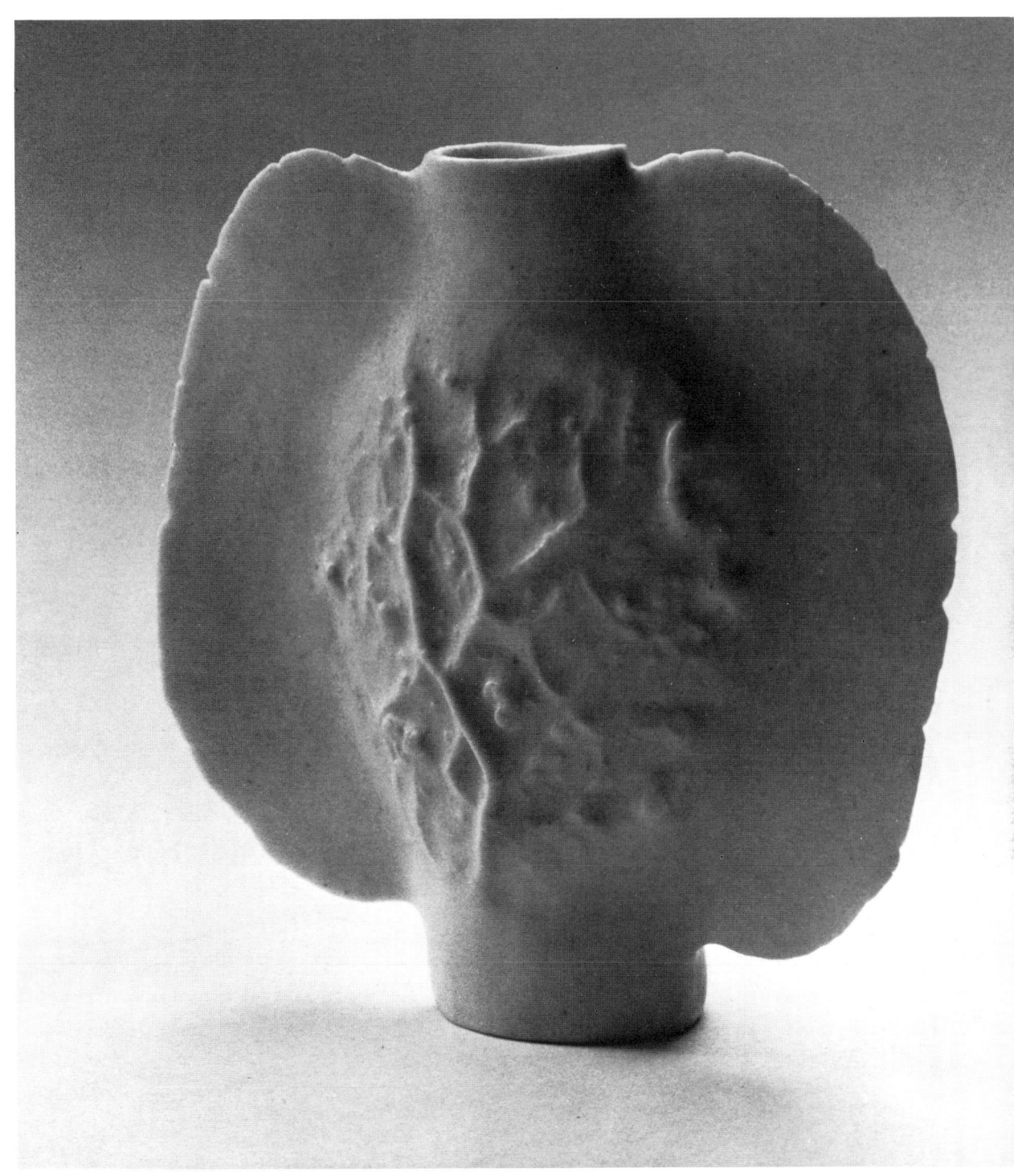

The pattern on this pot was made by impressing the wet clay surface with a roughly eroded pebble. 4 inches high, 1973.

2   Methods of pinch and coil-building

Types of clay

The actual methods of making by hand may be the same whichever clay one is using, and some ideas work equally well, though with differing qualities, in a variety of clays. But not all do: we usually find that some forms are better suited to the rock-like density of stoneware, some to the smooth delicacy of porcelain, and some to the warm earthiness of earthenware. To take an analogy from music—some tunes are better suited to being played on a cello, some on a piano and others on a flute. A love song is not at its most persuasive played on a drum, nor a lullaby on a trumpet. Potters have to suit their materials to their purpose and use them as sensitively as a composer uses his various instruments for different effects and moods. Admittedly, shock effects are possible by deliberately choosing to turn things on their heads, in the way that a fashion designer may choose to make a raincoat out of chiffon to draw greater attention to the current 'line' without reference to use, or else just for fun. Or a Dadaist may decide to make a fur-lined teacup. But things of this kind are transient joke products, where the very unsuitability of the material for its purpose *is* its purpose! But a joke generally loses its impact through repetition, relying for its effect mainly on its unexpectedness, and the exception merely proves the rule that there are

some things which are better made in one material than in another.

We can easily recognize the intended humour of the chiffon raincoat, or the surrealist's fur-lined teacup, because we already know what a raincoat and a teacup should be used for. In other words we can recognize suitability of material to purpose when the object has a practical use, as with domestic pottery. But if we are dealing with a piece of ceramic which has no particular function other than to translate into clay certain aspects of the world and to communicate our feelings through the material, and for this we choose a clay which fires with

Meret Oppenheim; 'Le Dejeuner en Fourrure'.

qualities at variance with the intention, we will merely make a confused and confusing image. Its impact will not be as intended, the idea will still be isolated in our minds, and we will fail to convey what we want through the object, either to ourselves or to anyone else. So, if we want to free the idea, and to get our point across, we must know the particular qualities possible with the clays and glazes with which we work, whatever means we use to form them. If the clay is not suitable for its purpose the whole idea will misfire, however well it may be made, and however good the idea.

So how do we decide?

Basically, of course, it is by continually making and experimenting, and then critically assessing the results. But there are ways of thinking which provide short cuts, and possibly save a great deal of fruitless work.

The two clays, stoneware and earthenware, clearly state by their very names what their fired qualities are. Fired stoneware is like stone, earthenware is like earth. Porcelain is a little more difficult to think of by this simple method, but not when its most likely derivation is known. 'Porcellana' is a derivative of the Italian *porcella*, which means cowrie shell. The cowrie, with its smooth, dense, perfectly formed and polished shell, and a feeling of depth through its 'glazed' surface, certainly does look as though it is made in porcelain (or that porcelain is made from it!) so the same word was used for both. Marco Polo, the Venetian, used the word 'porcellana' in the thirteenth century to describe Chinese porcelain when he recorded his travels through China. But the word does not seem to have been in general use in Europe until the sixteenth century. In fact so linked by then were the qualities of porcelain ware and those of the cowrie shell that, in 1516, Odoardo Barbosa of Lisbon, after having been on a journey to China, reported that crushed cowrie shells were the essential ingredient of porcelain![2] Incidentally, it does not appear that Marco Polo had thought this was the case.

His description, though not the entire story, was accurate and thorough, and clearly shows that he knew porcelain to be made of 'a certain kind of earth'.

Knowing that the word porcelain in effect means cowrie shell, it is obvious that delicate and precious shell-like qualities seem natural to porcelain, in the same way that stoneware has a strong stone-like appearance, and that fired earthenware has the warm look of sun-baked earth; and we can design with this simple set of analogies in mind.

Maturing clay

Before any pottery can be made successfully, the clay itself must be in the right condition. Its nature and plasticity will very largely determine the sort of forms that are possible.

Clay generally improves enormously from being left to mature, and this should be done for as long as possible. It has always been considered to be of benefit, as will be seen from this extract from *The Travels of Marco Polo*, written in the thirteenth century. When describing the porcelain-making centre of Tingui in China he says: '... cups or bowls and dishes of porcelain ware are there manufactured. The process was explained to be as follows. They collect a certain kind of earth, as it were, from a mine, and lay it in a great heap, suffer it to be exposed to the wind, the rain, and the sun, for thirty or forty years, during which time it is never disturbed. By this it becomes refined and fit for being wrought into the vessels above mentioned. Such colours as may be thought proper are then laid on, and the ware is afterwards baked in ovens or furnaces. Those persons, therefore, who cause the earth to be dug, collect it for their children and grandchildren.'[3]

Unfortunately we are unlikely to have such far-sighted grandparents! But a little keeping is better than none at all, even for the refined commercially produced clay bodies sold by pottery suppliers.

Wedging

The next stage of the preparation of the clay is to wedge it thoroughly. This will even out the plasticity, and also get rid of any air bubbles which may be in it. Wedging can be done by different methods. There is the cut and slam method and the spiral wedging method, which I personally always use. This Japanese method of rolling and lifting and then pressing the lump of clay rhythmically down and round into itself is both effective and satisfying. A piece of clay, either of a size estimated as being necessary for one pot, or a lump large enough for several pots, is held gently in position on the working-table top, and slowly rotated with the supporting hand whilst the heel of the other hand presses down and round again and again into the centre, so forming a spiralling shell-form. The movement goes down through the back, shoulders and arms and into the clay through the hands so that the clay turns round and back into itself as the natural culmination of the easy circular rocking movement. The Japanese call this method 'nejimomi', which means literally 'kneading by twisting', or 'kikumomi', which very poetically describes the form which the clay takes on, because it means 'Chrysanthemum wedging'.

For good hand-building it is often best to spiral-wedge each piece of clay individually, immediately before working with it. One is not dealing with large numbers when pinch-building, so there is no need to prepare a great deal of clay at one time. With porcelain especially, the pieces of prepared clay so quickly lose their essential plasticity that I find it best to proceed straight from the wedging to the shaping. Also this initial handling enables you to get to know the feel and character of the clay and allows time to clear and focus the mind, and to relax, ready for making the pot.

Very soon you begin to know, as you wedge your clay, what sort of form the clay will be happy to take. Whether or not, for example, to attempt a fairly large or difficult piece with that particular lump, or whether the plasticity is not so good, indicating that only small forms will be able to be pinched out of it. If it feels too sticky it will probably be best to put it by for a short while to dry out a little, or else to pinch it up only part way, thickly, and then to leave the half-made piece resting on its rim on a non-absorbent surface, and to do the final pinching out a little later when it has the right feel and is less tacky.

Condition of the clay

For good, easy and enjoyable pinching, the clay should be wedged until it will readily take the imprint of the fingers and thumb. With fine clay, such as porcelain, even the most delicate

A ball of clay which has been wedged, and is now in a good workable condition ready for pinching.

finger impressions should be able to be seen. The finger and thumb should leave the clay cleanly, with no adherence at all as the pinching takes place. There should be no need to press, just a gentle rhythmic series of squeezes should be all that is needed until the walls are nearly finished, by which time the clay will be found to have dried out considerably in the warmth of the hands. By this stage the walls can be squeezed quite hard without distorting the form. This natural drying out of the clay as it is worked upon can be a great help, because the walls will begin to hold a shape which would otherwise become unmanageable as they become larger. But it can be maddening if the correct shape has not been achieved before the clay loses its plasticity. Various things may cause this to happen, some preventable, others not. The clay may have been too 'short', that is, not plastic enough to begin with. The piece attempted may have been too large, or too complex, to be pinched out completely, so that some of the clay still waiting to be formed has dried out before it can be worked on. The pinching may be indecisive, and so the clay will be overhandled and therefore lose its plasticity. The atmosphere in the workroom may be too warm, which will cause premature drying out. Or there may be unavoidable outside interruptions before the work is finished. To anticipate inevitable inter-ruptions during the pinch-building I keep a few plastic bags, and varying-sized supports such as cups and dry sponges, close to me, so that the pot can quickly be put into the air-proof bag and then rested on the support until I am able to resume the pinching. The plasticity of the clay can sometimes be retained sufficiently, even for a few hours with the thicker-walled stoneware, but not for very long with thin-walled porcelain, unfortunately.

I find it best not to add water to the walls whilst they are being pinched out, though occasionally towards the end of the work I do dampen the fingers with which I am pinching. Water can give a false idea of the plasticity of the clay so that the pinching out will have the wrong pressure, and the walls tend to get slimy so that they distort and tear easily as they slip away from the pressure of the finger tips. If the clay is found to be too dry and lacking in plasticity when the pinching is started, it is much better to open it all out into a rough slab, sprinkle it with water, then roll it together again. It may be stored in a plastic bag for use later. Before attempting to use it again it will, of course, have to be thoroughly re-wedged.

Pinching

The best pace for the work to proceed at is one

The ball of clay is opened up with the thumb, forming a thick-walled hollow, as the cross-section BELOW *shows.*

of slow, relaxed concentration. Holding the ball of clay in one hand, gently push the thumb of the other hand towards its centre, slowly turning the ball of clay whilst this is being done. The pad of the thumb is used rather than the tip. Then, still rotating the clay, round out the base with the curve of the thumb. To a large extent the final form which the pot will be able to have is determined at this stage. It is the root-base from which the form will spring and grow, and so it must, at the beginning, be made the correct shape. If, for example, the pot is to be a sharply curving narrow-based form, this is most easily started, after the initial opening up, by inserting a finger of one hand into the hollow and then moulding the clay evenly over the rounded end of this finger with the pad of the thumb of the other hand. If it is to be widely curving and shallow then, after opening the form up initially, the clay is eased out gently into a wide base with the curve of the thumb. But whatever the shape, the base has to be pinched out to its final thinness right at the beginning, especially with a larger form. This is necessary because the length of the thumb is the maximum depth which can possibly be reached for pinching. If the walls are to be any deeper than this it is possible to modify the form to a certain extent at a later stage by putting the whole hand inside so that the pot hangs down over the wrist, then working over

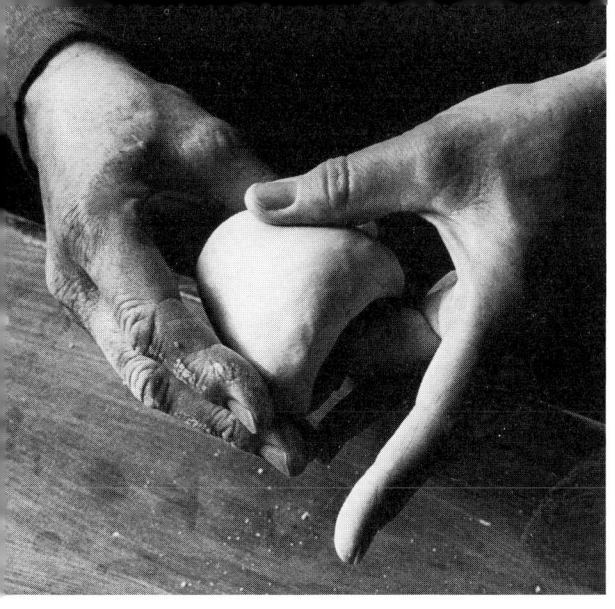

To give a steep-sided conical base, a finger is placed into the initial hollow and the clay is moulded over it. To give a wide-based curve the thumb is used to ease the clay out to the width and thickness required for the finished pot, as the cross-sections show. It is necessary to do this at an early stage because once the walls have been extended the thumb and finger can no longer reach the base.

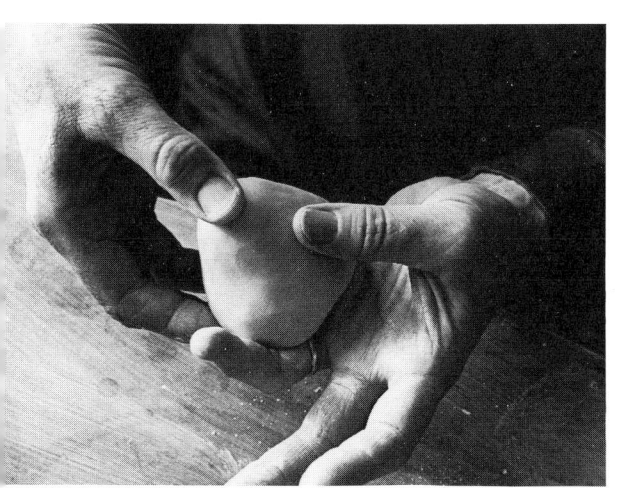

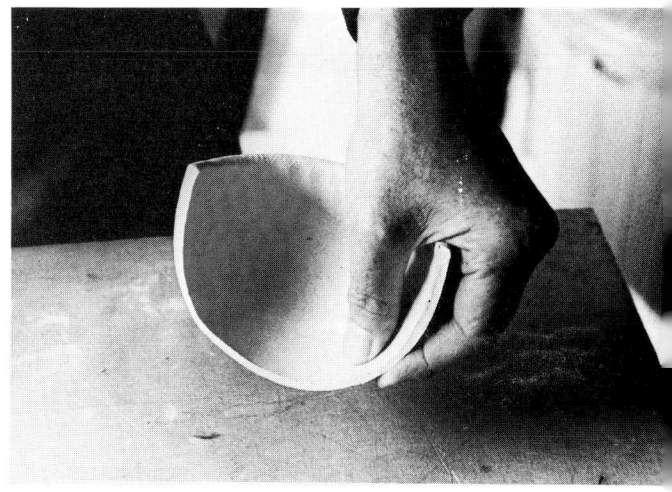

the outside with the thumb or fingers of the other hand. But this is rather awkward and unnecessary, as it can all be done more naturally at an early stage.

After having made the base, the walls are then gradually thinned and so raised upwards, with a circling series of pinches, gently pressing the clay between the finger and thumb, each higher ring of pinched depressions slightly overlapping the previous ones. The main aim is to keep the pressure between the finger and thumb even, and the spaces between each squeeze equal. The work proceeds slowly and rhythmically, and seems to grow with a natural inevitability. For a small shape, or a fairly thick one, one journey from

the base and around the walls to the rim may be sufficient. But if egg-shell thinness is being aimed at, as will probably be the case with porcelain, or if a larger piece is being made in any sort of clay, then there will have to be many rows of pressed indentations. These may then need to be worked over again, a second time, concentrating on pressing out the slightly raised ridges between the finger marks, and between the rows.

Finely pinched porcelain clay dries out quickly and stiffens while being handled during making. The heavier, thicker stoneware clays, however, do not, and so the walls of the pot may become very floppy as they become larger. It may then be found easier to

LEFT *To make a larger form the hand may be placed inside to act as a support, and the clay may be shaped over this with the fingers of the other hand.*

The clay wall is gradually thinned from base to top with slightly overlapping rows of rhythmic pinching, as shown in the cross-sections TOP, *until an even thickness is acquired throughout, as seen* RIGHT.

The series of cross-sections BELOW *shows how the small thick-walled pot becomes progressively thinner and larger as it is pinched.*

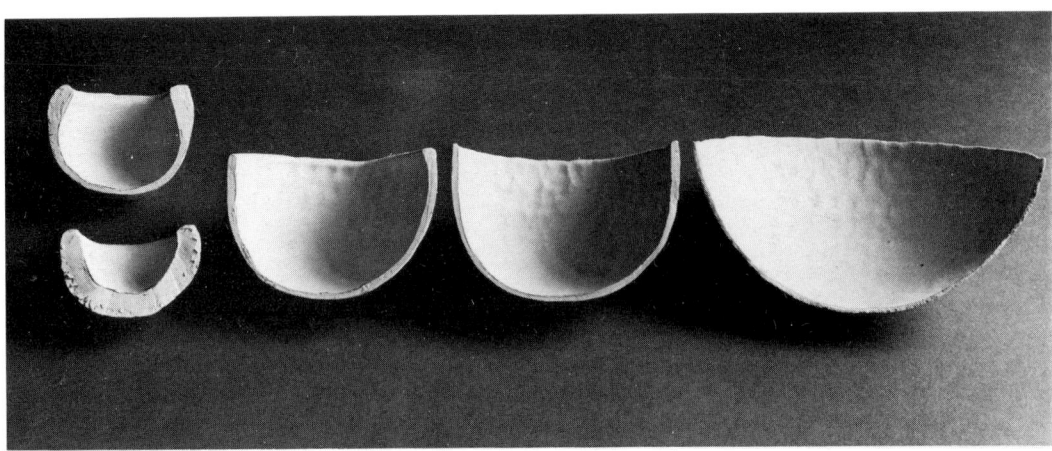

hold the growing shape on its side whilst working, and to support the soft floppy walls on the wrist of the supporting hand. Or, if this proves awkward, the piece may be left to rest on its rim to stiffen up a little before continuing. Thus it is often a good idea to work on two or three pots at a time, so that the rhythm of work is not lost whilst waiting for the piece to stiffen up and hold its shape unsupported.

When a fairly thick wall is being thinned out the excess clay may be smeared up the walls from the base to the top on both the inside and outside. This is a fairly rough method of smoothing out the bulk of the clay, and it will probably be found necessary to pinch all over the form once again to make walls of an even thickness.

If the pot is to have an inward-turning curve, then the top needs to be gently eased in—that is collared—between each row of pinching, to make it smaller. Inevitably this will cause slight creases and gathers, which must be welded together as the work progresses. With an outward-curving pot the clay is eased from the inside over and out, and the excess clay which gathers at the top will finally have to be pinched out to an even thinness.

The clay at the rim may be smoothed and pinched out more finely to give an undulating edge.

Rim

It will be found that the rim will inevitably have a certain unevenness or undulation as a natural result of the way in which the piece has grown. These slight variations are the natural termination of the irregular curvature of the walls and, if they turn out to be completely well-balanced and pleasing, they can be left as a distinctive and attractive feature of the pinch-built method. Indeed, these unrepeatable irregularities can be emphasized and made into an even more distinctive feature by being pinched out very finely, and allowed to split, bend and curl, further emphasizing the organic quality of the work. But if a more 'tidy' rim is preferred, or is a

Cutting off a ragged top with a needle

necessary design feature, the undulating, sometimes ragged, top edge may be cut off to give a clean curve or a straight top edge. This can be done with a needle, a blade, or even scissors. The raggedness of the cut clay should be smoothed out, as tactile pleasure is one of the delights of ceramics and a harsh, cutting edge usually feels wrong. A little water on the fingers may help in this final smoothing off.

What is important is that the rim, the place at which the outer form changes direction into the inner form, should look purposeful, however irregular and uneven it may be. It should not appear to be accidentally chipped or broken, but to be intended to be the way that it is, the inevitable termination of the curve of the walls and form of the pot.

In this invincible and one might say flawless progression of form, which involves and develops its whole setting according to the continuous fatality of its convolutions and seems to create its own time, we admire the combination of rhythm, *marked by the regular spots or spines, and of* indivisible movement. *It is like seeing music. The correspondence or ornaments on successive spirals suggests a counterpoint, while the continuity sustains the main theme of the rotation of the surface.*

But suddenly an end must come. This strange torsion must cease, the nacre on the inside and the coarser covering must join, and the distinction between the two substances of the shell must vanish or explain itself, while at the same time its form must be completed by some decision that remains to be arrived at.

The problem is very general in kind. Living nature must solve it in all the types it displays, all of which involve extremities to be modelled and cavities or tubes that must be made to reach the outside world. The mind staggers at the mere thought of analyzing the innumerable solutions it has found. . . . She knows how to finish a plant, how to open nostrils, a mouth, a vulva, how to create a setting for an eyeball; she thinks suddenly of the sea shell when she has to unfold the pavilion of an ear, which she seems to fashion the more intricately as the species is more alert.

Actually, even the mathematician is baffled when in the end the tube suddenly broadens, breaks, curls back, and overflows into uneven lips, which part as though made of flesh, disclosing in a fold of the softest mother-of-pearl the smoothly inclined starting point of an internal whorl that recedes into darkness.

'Man and the Sea Shell' from Aesthetics *by Paul Valéry*

71

Supports

When the main form is finished it may still be too soft to hold its own shape without some sort of support. These supports may be improvised in many different ways. Basically the shape must either be rested in, or over something, or be propped up by something. The important thing is that whatever support is used it must not be of a shape which will press into the clay whilst it is drying out, otherwise the shape and the surface may be dented or deformed.

If a rounded pot with an outward-curving rim has been made, and it is firm enough not to slump, it may be rested in something such as a cup with an outward-flaring lip which will not dig into the soft clay wall. If the entire pot is too soft to hold its own shape, including the base, it is best to hang it over something round, such as a ball. This ball—varying-sized children's balls are ideal—should be covered with a piece of cloth, such as an old nylon stocking, to prevent the clay from sticking to it. The pot should hang loosely over the support and be removed as soon as the clay becomes firm, otherwise as it dries out and contracts it will cling to the supporting ball, and be difficult, or even impossible, to remove from the support. If the pot is straight-sided, or inward-curving, it may be rested in any bowl which roughly approximates to its dimensions, being propped up if necessary by pieces of plastic foam between it and the sides of the bowl. This is also a useful way of supporting a very irregular shape. It can be held inside a bowl large enough to contain it comfortably with any irregularities and protruding parts of the modelling supported by specially made props of plastic foam. Sometimes I drape a criss-cross of strips cut from lightweight polythene bags across the inside of the supporting bowl, so that the pot may be easily lifted out by using these as sling supports. If an upright columnar shape has been made, or if a wide overhang is part of the design, I once again find that variously shaped

The base of a pot may be supported in a cup whilst it is stiffening, or, when the walls are still floppy, it may be hung over a nylon-covered ball, as shown in the lower picture.

pieces of foam will act as a supporting 'scaffolding' whilst it is drying out. If a piece is firm enough to hold its own shape because it has dried out sufficiently during its making, but is still damp enough for the base curve to become depressed by its own weight, then I stand it on a *dry* sponge with a certain amount of give, rather than on a hard surface, until the base is firm enough to hold the weight completely.

Making footrings

Pots which are complete in themselves without the addition of a footring, usually stand better after firing if the base has been slightly hollowed out or dimpled. This is done by easing the base inwards with the finger, if the clay is still soft enough, or by scraping or carving out a small depression when it is dry. This will be found to be a wise precaution because a slight swelling can occur underneath the pot, where it rests on the shelf during the firing, and this may make the pot rock instead of standing firmly after it has been fired.

Assessing the size and position of the footring before it is joined to the pot.

If a footring is to be added to give 'lift' and 'spring' to the pot, and to complete the form, it is usually added when the pot is leather-hard. The ring is made by rolling, pinching or patting out a small lump of the clay into a strip. This strip is then cut to the right depth and length to be formed into a circle of suitable proportions for the footring of the pot. I have found that a quick method for judging the best size for a footring is to keep a collection of separate rings of differing sizes, and to try out the pot on top of these before cutting out the clay. These mock footrings are a mixed collection of the cardboard centres of such things as sticky tape, rolls of thread, or fired unglazed footrings from failed pots. These latter are also useful for propping up pieces in the kiln should they need support—naturally they must only touch unglazed areas of pots, otherwise they would fuse on to the surface.

73

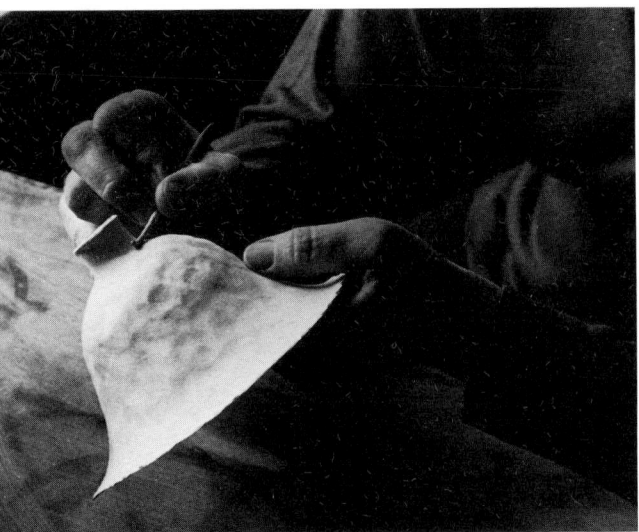

The position of the footring is marked on the base of the pot. It is then fixed on with slurry, and the joint is further strengthened with a little extra clay, which is smoothed in with a modelling tool.

When the size of the footring has been decided, the strip of clay is cut with mitred ends. This is formed into a circle by joining the ends together with slurry.

Slurry

Always use a slurry made from the same clay as that on which it is to be used. Dried out scraps and off-cuts do very well powdered up and mixed with water to a muddy consistency. It is found that powdered clay mixes much more readily with water than does plastic clay. For this reason, and so as not to lose the flow of the work by having to prepare some dry clay to make into a powder each time slurry is needed, I find it useful to keep labelled buckets of off-cuts and scrapings of each type of clay, ready to be turned into slurry when there is the need to join one piece of clay to another.

Fitting the footring to the pot

Because of the slight asymmetry of a hand-built pot the best point of balance is not necessarily in the centre of the base, and slight adjustments, by eye, will have to be made until the pot sits well. When the best place for the footring has been judged, by balancing the pot upon it in various positions, this place is marked on the base with a pencil or a point of some sort. Then slurry is dabbed on the top edge of the footring which is then gently pressed on to the marked place on the base of the pot. The clay from the pot is eased downwards into the clay of the footring with a wooden modelling tool, and that of the footring upwards into the clay of the pot, both inside and outside the circle of the footring. Small rolls of very plastic clay may be added around the joints. These additional rolls of clay may be considered necessary to strengthen the joint, to give a better curve to the profile, or to add a little extra weight to the base of the pot and so give it the added stability which may be required in a widely flaring form of delicate lightweight porcelain. If these small rolls of clay are to be added, they are once again eased up into the pot and down into the footring, using a wooden modelling tool. I find that using the fingers slightly dampened makes for a good final finish to the transitional curve from the foot into the body. Also you are then able to 'pull-out' the footring a little if this is found to be necessary in order to improve its curvature and thickness.

The whole pot is now left to become leather-hard in the case of stoneware, and completely dry in the case of porcelain, so that it is ready for the next stage.

Finishing off

The degree of finish of the completed work is determined by the qualities aimed at and by what is suitable for the type of clay which is being used. A pinch-built pot inevitably has a more or less indented surface where the fingers have left their impression. This broken surface texture may be left if it happens in a decorative or expressive manner, and does not seem merely arbitrary or accidental and detract from the appearance of the pot. In hand-built raku, for example, the total immediacy of the making and firing cycle may be carried through the whole piece so that all the marks showing the method of its making are left on the surface and look just right. Again, a rough-hewn, rock-like look can be in keeping with coarse-grained, heavily grogged stoneware, and so the surface marks which help to give the piece its rough quality may be counted as a desirable feature.

But porcelain, with its potential for the perfection of form and smoothness of surface of, say, a cowrie shell, is I think at its most sensually pleasing, both to look at and to handle, with a smooth, highly refined finish. Porcelain forms seem to me to be at their best when they are full and rich in form like a healthy fruit, and not dented or collapsed like a deflating balloon. Even slender forms can be 'full'. On forms of this kind the indentations of the finger marks can be too intrusive. They catch the light in an unintended way, especially on a glazed form, and by distracting the eye, they detract from our appreciation of the full sweep of the form. Also, there is for me a sense in which the object should be independent and self-contained and seem to have emerged or grown inevitably. Thus I prefer not to see too much the imprint of the maker, left as too-obvious finger indentations, which can be a sort of arrogance, like a massive signature drawing attention to itself on a painting.

Another thing which has to be borne in mind is the thickness of the intended glaze, and its consequent masking capacity. When it is thick the glaze will flow over and soften small marks on the surface, but the delicate coating of glaze which is applied to thin porcelain will mask very little.

If it is decided to perfect and clean up the form by scraping, this may be done with metal 'kidneys', which are flexible and sold with a variety of curves which will be found to accommodate most forms. Scrapers may of course be improvised from any material which is hard and smooth, and has some degree of

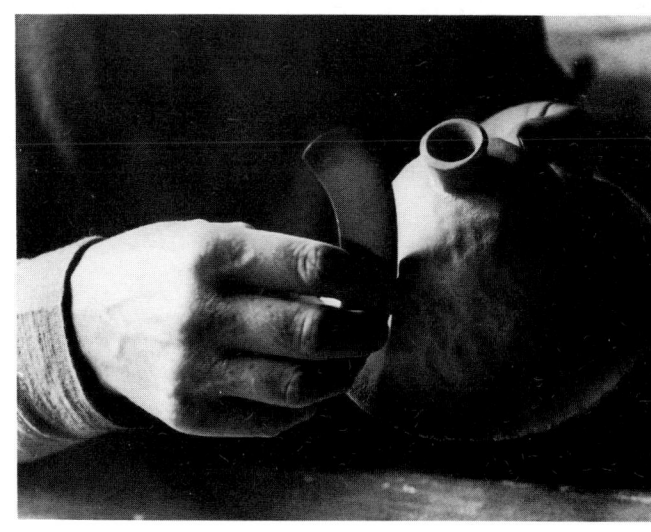

Refining the outer surface with a metal kidney

75

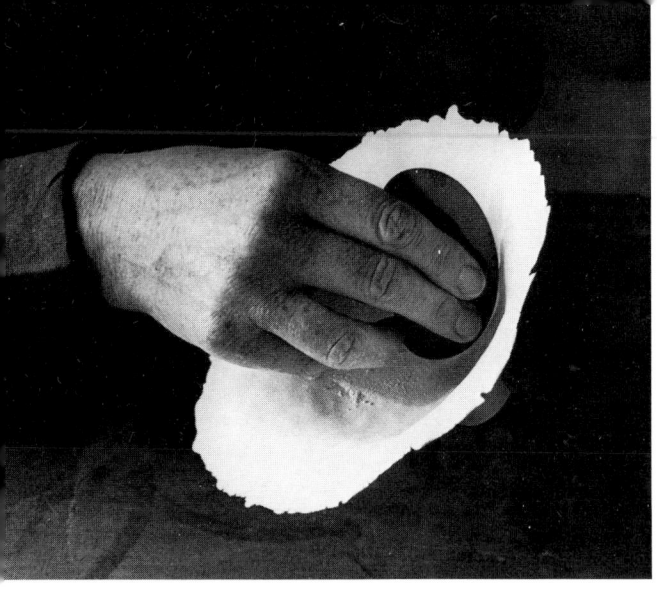

With the pot held in the palm of one hand the inner curve is gently scraped with the kidney.

flexibility. For example, African hand-builders use shaped pieces of calabash and gourd, and at the Herculaneum factory in Liverpool in 1827 it was noted by a visitor that, 'A piece of thin horn was used for shaping and polishing and finishing and also for press-moulding.'[4]

A face mask should be worn during this stage of the work, because of the clay dust which is created. This is very fine and floats in the air, and if inhaled over a period may damage one's health. I use a smog mask of the kind which can be bought at any chemists. They have replaceable pads which are sold separately. These masks are now also available from pottery suppliers. When working in a very dust-laden atmosphere it is sensible to wear nylon overalls so that the dust does not penetrate and build up in the fibres of your clothing. When scraping dry clay I personally work over a piece of plastic sheeting, and collect and dispose of the fine dust frequently.

You can be fairly rough when scraping leather-hard stoneware clays. In fact, if large amounts of clay need to be removed a piece of hacksaw blade makes a good tool. But with dry porcelain clay the pot needs to be held very gently whilst scraping is being done. I find that it is best to leave the porcelain until it is completely dry before I scrape it, despite its fragility, because at the leather-hard stage, owing to the clay's extreme smoothness and lack of 'bite', all that happens as a result of scraping is a series of facets on the surface of the form. This is, of course, quite the opposite of what one is attempting to do. Moreover, when it is thin and leather-hard a porcelain form is very easily bent whilst being held and scraped, so that it cracks readily under even the slightest pressure. I therefore find it best with delicate forms to work against the completely rigid, dried-out surface. You are then able to gauge exactly how much pressure you can safely put on the walls. In fact with porcelain the pressure must be no more than you would use if you were holding an empty egg-shell!

Coil-building

A pinch-pot, or thumb-pot, as it is often called, is obviously limited in size to the size of the hand, or hands. But there are extensions of pinch-building, which are really combination methods, by which larger and more complex forms can be made. Coil-building, except for those few pots in which the coils are merely laid one on top of the other without being blended together very much, is really a combination of coiling and pinching.

Usually the base of a coiled pot is made first, then the walls are built on this by the addition of rolls of clay, laid round and round, one on top of the other, and pinched and smeared together to make a unified surface. This process of coiling, smearing and pinching is repeated until the right size and shape have been achieved.

There are extremes in the methods of making coil-pots which extend from the obsessively careful to the wildly slap-happy. All the various styles of working have their place if they suit the maker, the nature of the clay which is being used, and eventually produce a good pot.

Coil-building of a very painstaking kind is started on a base which has been made from a carefully rolled out and precisely cut disc of clay. Then the rolls of clay, which will be coiled round to form the walls, are prepared by rolling out identical 'snakes', or ropes, between both hands on top of a dampish, or at least not too absorbent, surface. Quite a number of these clay ropes will be made at a time, and placed under a damp cloth or a piece of polythene to keep them in a suitably plastic condition until needed. One of these ropes of clay is then placed around the edge of the base, and then another on top of this and so on. Each row is painstakingly smoothed into the one below, before the next one is started, even joining the two ends of each complete circular coil together with a mitred finish. This careful process is continued until the whole pot has been completely formed.

At the other extreme of techniques in coil-building, great wads of clay are used and roughly smeared together upwards, from the base and over the inside walls with the whole hand. The outside is also welded together in a similar manner. More coils, maybe as thick as an arm, are joined to the growing form in a like manner until the required size has been achieved. The whole thick pot may then be beaten out to make the walls thinner and stronger.

The method used depends on such things as the plasticity of the clay, the size and roughness of the pot being made, the local

The coils which will be used to build the pot may be either rolled or pinched out to size.

traditions, the temperament of the maker and the size and conditions of the working area. The roughly made, frequently large, pieces are often built outside in the open air in warm regions where a large thick-walled pot in a coarse sticky clay is able to dry out quickly. The meticulous procedure is most suitable for small-sized precise work made with refined clays within a limited working area.

I personally like to make coiled pots by a method somewhere between these two extremes, and find that satisfying quick and fairly controlled results can be obtained, even for beginners, by the following methods.

First I start with a fairly rough and thick-walled pinch-pot. Then the first coil is added to this at what is, in fact, a small distance up the wall of the pot. I then form the coils by pinching them fairly roughly out of a lump of clay, letting the rope so formed hang downwards as it grows longer. This is then caught up in the hand, and joined to the top edge of the pinched base. If a large form is being made the coil will naturally be very long, and it is comfortable to let it lie along the wrist and forearm for support whilst it is being fed on to the pot. Each roll of clay is added with a slightly spiralling action, the thumb of the supporting and modelling hand smearing it in as it is gently pushed into place. After not more than two or three rows are eased into place, they must be smeared thoroughly downwards into the previous row, stroking and welding the clay firmly in more than one direction. The same method of smearing and welding the coils is used on the inside and outside. This rough wall is then pinched out to its final thinness, except for the top edge, which is left fairly thick, so as to leave enough clay to weld it to the next coil. It might be necessary to rest the inverted pot on a non-absorbent surface to stiffen up a little before any more coils are added. Then another two or three more rows are joined on and welded together to make a unified wall in the same way, proceeding until the entire form has been completed. In this way a very secure wall is

The pinched-out base is rested on a piece of dry sponge while the first coil is fed on and gently pressed into place. After every second or third coil the clay is welded firmly together on both the inside and outside, and is then pinched out evenly. Every so often the pot may be left, inverted on its rim, to stiffen up a little.

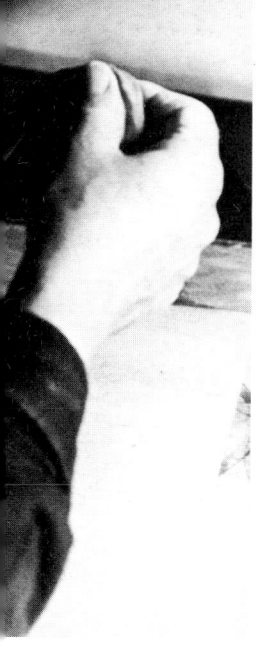

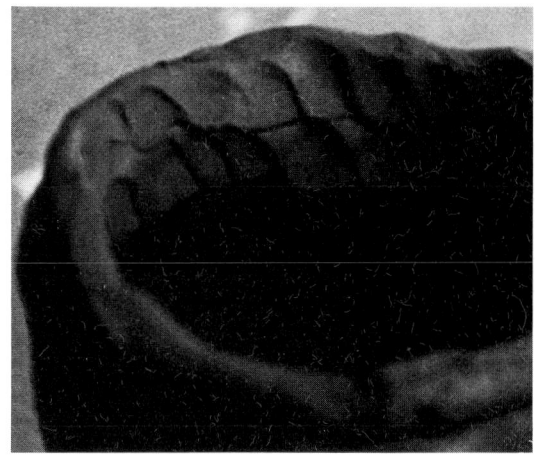

created, which does not open out along the coiling rings during the subsequent firing. Also, as a result of adding the first coil part of the way up the wall of a pinched hemisphere rather than to a flat disc, the potential weakness of the join at the angle of the base is avoided.

If an outward-swelling form is being made each coil is put a little to the outer edge of the previous one, and the welding, smearing and pinching is done to ease the form outwards. If the shape is an inward-turning one then the reverse is done, placing the coils a little to the inside, and easing them inwards with the smearing and pinching. The walls may, of course, be either thin or chunky, according to how much pinching is done.

If the asymmetrical tendency of the growing pot begins to give an unbalanced form, this can be rectified by using a beater to slap, or ease, the pot into a better shape. A hand is placed inside the form, to provide a support against which the beating is done. Or, should a collapsing shape need to be fattened out, the outside is supported whilst some suitable long-handled tool with a rounded end is used to beat out the depression or dent. It is easy to improvise something for this such as a wooden ball fixed to a stick. I use large spoons for the purpose, and find that they suit very well. An effective method of fattening out a rounded shape, so long as it is still flexible enough and not too dried out, is to blow into it. This will only work if the shape has a small opening, or one which can be temporarily closed in, as the air needs to be trapped inside for long enough to swell out the form.

The final finishing off and refinement of the form, including the perfecting of features like the change of direction from one curve to another at such places as the junction of the foot with the body, or the curve of the lip and rim, are effected in exactly the same way as with a totally pinch-built pot, that is by using metal kidneys, or similar tools, as scrapers. These can be used to tidy up both the outside and the inside of the pot, but if the form closes in to a narrow neck, it will be necessary to use a long slender tool for the inside, such as a wire tool or a griffon. These plaster-worker's 'griffons' are tougher than wire tools and their curved serrated ends are very useful for smoothing off the insides of difficult forms.

Inevitable asymmetry

With a hand-modelled pot, whether it is directly pinched from one ball of clay or built up coil upon coil, there will inevitably be a slight asymmetry in the form, in both the curvature of the walls and the unevenness and undulation of the rim. This is the natural result of the way in which the piece has grown. Each hand-modelled pot will vary from the next in the same way that each fruit in a group of apples or oranges will vary. We would call them all 'round', but when seen against a geometrically perfect sphere we recognize their individual variations. Geometric forms may satisfy the intellect, but organically varied ones are more pleasing to the senses. Most people find the variety and irregularity of the shapes of a group of apples more engaging than the sameness and geometrical perfection of a group of billiard or ping-pong balls.

A feeling for organic qualities in art and craft objects is usually associated with a feeling of close affinity with the natural world. It seems to have been most intense and deeply rooted in the Far East where it has had a strong religious and philosophical basis. The beautiful ease and naturalness of Japanese hand-modelled tea-bowls most perfectly embody an acceptance of natural unforced asymmetry which is neither deliberately avoided nor consciously sought after, but is accepted wherever it occurs naturally. This free attitude to form is beautifully realized in the hand-modelled Raku tea-bowls of such artists as Chojiro and Koetsu. It seems that around 1576, under the guidance of the tea master, Rikyu, Chojiro made the first hand-modelled

The four balls show the geometrical regularity and the sameness of machine-produced forms. The apples have the organic asymmetry and variety of natural growing forms.

Teabowls. TOP *Red Raku ware, 'Shunkan', by Chojiro.* ABOVE
'Mount Fuji' by Koetsu. BELOW *'Ayame' by Chojiro.*

Raku tea-bowls, thus inaugurating a style of work which reached a peak of expressiveness in the bowls of Koetsu (1558–1637), which most harmoniously combine a lively inventiveness with refined tranquillity. An interesting account of a similar attitude to asymmetry is given by Soetsu Yanagi in *The Unknown Craftsman.*[5] He describes how the wooden bowls of Korea are turned from sap-green wood, even though sooner or later they will almost certainly bend and split. But this progressive distortion of the forms, as the wood dries out, is simply accepted with no feeling that the bowls are spoiled by it.

The reason for the slight asymmetries of hand-built pottery lies in the way in which they are formed from the very outset. The lump of clay which is to become the pot is first patted only approximately into a sphere, and then the thumb enters and opens up this form only more or less centrally. In this way slight variations of rim curvature and wall height are determined from the very start by accidental and unpredictable differences in the thickness of the clay around the central hollow. This tendency to asymmetry then continues throughout the whole forming process, because the developing shape is not rotated around a fixed centre, but is moved freely in the palm of the hand. This is in direct contrast to the process of throwing on the wheel, in which a high degree of symmetry is ensured, first by the exact centering of the clay on the wheelhead, then by forming this into a perfect dome and opening it up exactly centrally. Continuing with the spin of the wheel, the form is then given its hollow shape and volume around a central axis, so ensuring symmetry of form and profile. Admittedly wheel-thrown forms each differ from the next in a way that slip-cast pieces from the same mould do not, but they have, by their very nature, to conform to the law of centrifugal force, and rotation about a fixed axis, which is not the case with hand-held, hand-formed pieces. So, to gain the maximum value from the different process of hand-building, a

BELOW *Pinched bowl, 4½ inches diameter, 1974.*

certain amount of organic asymmetry in the
form should be accepted as an inevitable part
of its character.

3

Inbuilt colour and decoration

With coiling and pinching, either used separately or combined, a great many elaborations of the form can be built in as the work progresses. The possibility for experimentation is endless. As different things are tried out each new idea breeds others with a recognizable family likeness, so that each single idea branches out into other related experiments, like an extensive family tree. The imagination becomes full of more and more possibilities for new forms and decorations, each one related to the source, but maybe with only a hint of the original starting point. Not only does the 'vocabulary' of forms and patterns grow as each idea is allowed to branch out into new areas, but also the technical ability for actually realizing these ideas increases. Each problem solved adds to the fund of skill, so that there is an increasing amount to be tapped and blended together, with endless permutations. In this way true originality and progression can occur in a person's work. Not in the sense, necessarily, of progressively better work, but of work flowing with a sense of unified style and direction. No two people have the same infinitely complex set of experiences, both inside and outside their working pattern. Thus the same translation of an idea into materials cannot take place honestly. Each mature artist's work tends to develop a character of its own.

As you work, and can see many fascinating paths for experimentation branching out, you realize that each choice of direction means foregoing other equally valid ones, which there will not be the time to pursue. And you may realize that some aspect which now absorbs you for the first time in the course of the new developments of the work may be at variance with ideas which you previously had felt to be acceptable.

A close questioning observation of the structure of the world is particularly likely among craftsmen who work with natural materials, and every potter uses the most basic natural materials. Earth, water, rocks and metals are all combined by the potter himself to make forms of his own imagination. And he then makes these invented forms permanent by the use of fire, in much the same way that rocks themselves are formed.

In searching for natural materials in the ground, the imagination may be stirred in many ways. The potter Bernard Palissy (1510–89), who made such strangely modern looking wares 400 years ago, was a man whose enquiring mind went further than just looking in the ground for his materials for use. Through his close observations he insisted that the fossils which he found in the rocks around his home at Saintes in France were the remains of animals, plants and sea-creatures from long ago. He put forward these ideas in

Dish with astonishingly naturalistic modelled decoration by Bernard Palissy. Lead glaze, 21 inches across.

lectures which he gave in Paris in 1575, and he also published his theories in 1563 and 1580.* 'When that I had regarded well the shapes of these stones, I found that none could assume the form of a shell nor of any other creature, except the animal itself had shaped it . . . I maintain that the petrified fishes found in certain quarries have been engendered in that very spot, while the rocks were yet but water and mud, and which have since become petrified with the aforesaid fishes . . .'.[6]

Before that, during the Middle Ages, and indeed well into the nineteenth century, the presence of fossils was usually accounted for by mysterious mythological or religious explanations.

An awareness of the geological origins of his raw material is part of the potter's stock-in-trade, even though many may nowadays

Récepte Véritable by Bernard Palissy, 1563. *Discours Admirables* by Bernard Palissy, 1580.

buy raw materials ready packaged. There are still some pleasant communities which dig, grind, and mix and blend all of their materials, and a few tireless modern stalwarts may continue to do so for the totality of the experience and the satisfaction that it gives to them. But, packaged or dug, the raw materials still need to be selected, mixed and combined by the potter, and even when working with ready labelled bags of pulverized rocks and clays and other minerals, their geological origins may be just as potent a stimulation to the imagination.

One effect of this geological interest may be to make us aware of rocks as a potential source of design, both in their form and textures, and in their coloration, which is caused by the presence of metallic oxides. As far as I was concerned it was the need, at one stage of my work, to find clays which, when fired, had the look of rocks—of granite, sandstone and slate

Inspiration can come from fossils in rock or banding in water-worn pebbles. The stoneware pebble pot BELOW RIGHT *was coiled and inlayed with light-coloured bands. Unglazed, oxidized, 1280°C, 4 inches diameter, 1961.*

for example—which led me to experiment with adding oxides to clays. I felt the need to make a substance which was coloured right through, as a rock is, not just coloured on the surface. At first I noticed the ways in which pebbles often have a banded striped pattern running right through them. These pebble forms, with their subtle asymmetries and variations, seemed to me to be particularly well suited to the quality of the forms which can be made by coiling and pinching methods.

Most people enjoy collecting pebbles on the beach, and it is with exactly the same, possibly unconscious critical senses that we assess a good hand-built pot as we do a 'good' pebble. Among the pebbles which catch the eye immediately, some do not satisfy our sense of balance when picked up, or sit well in the hand, while others do. These 'good' ones are

A small pinched or coiled pot may be worked on all round, in a fully three-dimensional manner. It may be held and turned in the hands.

often kept and treasured. What they have that makes them attractive is a special combination of looks, balance, weight, form and texture. To digress, one wonders whether 'primitive' tribes, who have so often excelled at hand-built pottery, have done so to some extent because they are in constant touch—quite literally—with natural objects through using and working with them in their daily lives. A good hand-built pot—any pot, in fact, however it is made—should not only appeal immediately to the eye, but should make you want to pick it up, and should then reveal qualities which satisfy the senses of touch and balance. A small pinched or coiled pot can be a fully three-dimensional form, because of the way in which it is made in the hands, with no need to be held down to a base line during the making. It has no up or down, no front or back, but is fully in the round at all stages.

Clay coloration

Natural raw clays occur in a wide range of colours, from white through buffs and browns to deep red, and in various shades of grey to almost black. Much of this colour, however, is due to the presence of organic matter which burns away during a firing, leaving a pale body which often lacks character, especially after an oxidized firing. But when the colour is due to the presence of metallic oxides such as

iron oxide the colour is retained, and may even become richer after firing, the depth of colour varying with the amount of oxide present. This led me to experiment by adding other oxides to clay bodies in order to get a range of coloured clays in oxidized firing conditions. In reduction firing, clay bodies are more likely to fire with a richer and more interesting range of colours without much help from the potter.

The actual method of colouring the clay right through with oxides is very simple. But experiments with one's own clay and firing conditions should be undertaken first to get an idea of the way in which the clay behaves when it has been oxided. Too much oxide can bring the maturing temperature of the body down to a surprising extent. In my early untutored experiments I have known oxided clay to melt and run down over the kiln shelves, and actually eat deeply into the floor of the kiln! The culprit in this particular case was an excess of manganese.

It is salutory to know that the indefatigable giant amongst potter-experimentors, Josiah Wedgwood (1730–95), made thousands of tests over a long period before he perfected his Jasper Ware, which was introduced around 1775. It is interesting to muse, also, that he was attempting to get clays which were coloured right through with the same qualities as natural stones and rocks, and that he called them by the names of these rocks and stones—

Jasper, Basalt and Agate. But before this, in 1708, Johann Friedrich Böttger (1682–1719)—not a potter but an alchemist—was actually engaged in trying to find methods of manufacturing precious stones by the fusion at high temperatures of natural earths and minerals. Through these experiments he made his famous stoneware, which he called 'Jasper' and which could be cut and polished as though it were a true semi-precious stone, and can easily be mistaken for natural red Jasper. It puts ones own experiments in perspective, and also gives a good feeling of continuity to know that the same sort of excitement and questing recur, however different in quality and scale the results of our personal rediscoveries may be.

Mixed oxided clays

I find that the best way of obtaining even coloration is to add the measured powdered oxides to the measured out powdered clays. However well wedged the clay may be, it is difficult to obtain an even coloration by adding oxides when it is plastic. The clay may be clay waste, that is off-cuts and scraps from previous work, and it should all be of one type, not a mixture of clays with different firing properties. This is another occasion when the labelled bins of off-cuts and shavings left over from working with various clays come in useful, in the same way that they do for making slurry. All the pieces of dried out clay are ground up between sheets of tough paper, with a rolling pin, until they become an evenly textured powder. A measured quantity of this powder is then collected in a bucket or a large bowl, the right proportion of powdered oxide is sprinkled on to it, and water is then added.

I have found the following proportions of oxides for colouring clay bodies satisfactory. All are suited for white-firing stoneware clays firing at temperatures of around 1260°C in an oxidizing atmosphere. Grog in the suggested amount of 1 part may be added to all the recipes to give texture and strength. White grog will show up well on the deeper firing bodies. All materials are measured in parts by volume.

black iron oxide	1	*gives grey/*
clay (powdered)	40	*brown*
copper carbonate	1	*gives pale*
clay (powdered)	40	*grey/green*
red iron oxide	1	*gives warm*
clay (powdered)	20	*golden/brown*
cobalt carbonate	1	*gives deep*
clay (powdered)	40	*purple/grey/blue*
manganese dioxide	1	*gives metallic*
clay (powdered)	50	*speckles*

To get even more subtle colours use more than one oxide:

cobalt carbonate	1
manganese dioxide	1
clay (powdered)	100
red iron oxide	1
manganese dioxide	1
clay (powdered)	80
red iron oxide	3
manganese dioxide	1
clay (powdered)	80
black iron oxide	1
manganese dioxide	1
clay (powdered)	80
cobalt carbonate	1
manganese dioxide	2
clay (powdered)	150
cobalt carbonate	1
red iron oxide	1
clay (powdered)	120

All the above mixtures will give, when fired, clays which resemble natural rocks—granite, slate and sandstone, for example. To get such colours as pinks, yellows and oranges there are now many body stains available from pottery suppliers, and their catalogues give instructions as to their use.

Although the oxides are already powdered I usually grind them in the same way as the powdered clay in order to remove any large grains. With many oxides these give rise to an unpleasant uneven speckling. In the case of manganese oxide, however, the uneven speckling is an attractive feature, and grinding is not necessary.

When the powdered clays and oxides are all mixed up together evenly, I add slowly to this mixture a quantity of water. Rain-water is best as it gives better plasticity to the clay mixture. As much water should be added as is necessary to soak all the powder. It does not matter if too much water is added at this stage, because when the clay has settled and absorbed all that it can of the water, the excess liquid can be scooped off with a cup or jug, or siphoned off the top. When there is a well-blended muddy mixture in the bucket, with no dry areas at all, I turn it all out on an absorbent surface. I prefer wood, but if plaster bats are used they should first be covered with a thin cloth to avoid picking up plaster chips with the clay. The covering does not lessen the absorbency of the plaster surface, but it might prevent 'blow outs' in the kiln. Then the sticky mass should be turned frequently in order to dry it out. The idea is obviously to dry the mixture evenly by letting the air get to as much of the surface as possible. So, when it is not too sticky to handle, I loop it into a series of arched sausage shapes whose surface areas I enlarge by making dents all over with the fingers and thumb. Then, when it is soft but not sticky, I spiral-wedge it. Each differently coloured clay is then put into a polythene bag which is clearly labelled with the exact proportions of clay to oxide which have been used, and also a rough note of its fired colour, such as pale

brown seeds squeezed on overlaid on white fretting.

grey/blue, speckled buff/brown. Black pencil or waterproof ink is obviously best for this as polythene gets sweaty and damp with the plastic clay in it, and the labels get smudged and illegible if written in ordinary ink. For the really well-organized potter tags of fired clay made of each mixture may be tied on the appropriate bag, to show exactly how each coloured clay will appear when fired. I find that clays will keep in a good workable condition for years in well-sealed polythene bags; in fact they improve with ageing. I usually keep the bags of plastic clay in dustbins as an added precaution against air getting in and drying it out.

Since clay reclamation is a regular part of workshop routine it makes good sense to use it as an opportunity to gain an entirely different clay. Obviously, for the sort of workshop where large amounts of clay are used, such as one making a great deal of domestic wheel-thrown ware, a pug-mill may be considered a necessity. But with hand-building of the pinched and coiled variety there is not usually a great deal of wastage and so the reclamation of clay is likely to be on a small scale, and can be done by hand.

Grog

When I was studying the structure of rocks and pebbles and experimenting to produce clays which would have some of their qualities, I noticed that some of the coloured bands in pebbles were not only of a different colour, but were also rougher or smoother in texture than the main body. This suggested that additions to the basic clay body need not be confined to colouring oxides, but could also include some rough particles, or grog, to give this added interest of surface.

Grog, of course, is added not only to give texture to a body, but for purely practical reasons as well. It is used to improve the strength and drying out properties of the clay, particularly in large work. It can also improve

The pots LEFT *and* BELOW *were each made from two separately pinched and joined elements. The interior hollow was revealed by carving, or else by peeling back the top section, and within this 'seeds' made from clays of a different colour were placed and fixed either with slurry or with glaze.* LEFT *$2\frac{1}{2}$ inches diameter, 1970;* BELOW *4 inches long, 1972.*

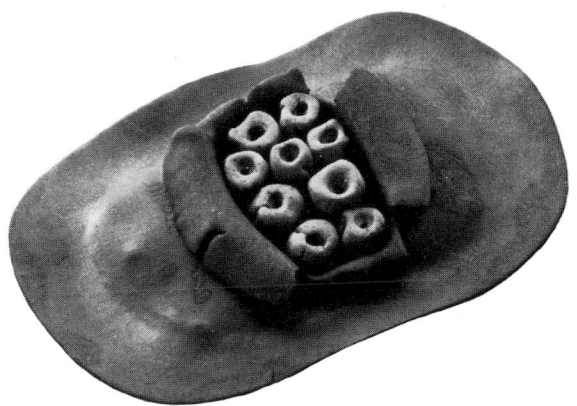

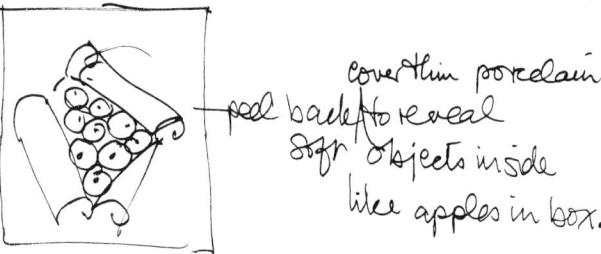

cover thin porcelain
peel back to reveal
soft objects inside
like apples in box.

the handling properties of a too smooth and dense clay, 'opening it up' and making it easier to work with. Grog may be made by the individual potter to suit particular needs, or it can be bought from pottery suppliers in a variety of grain sizes and colours, if this is more convenient. The types available are well described in pottery catalogues. The higher the mesh number the finer the grain size—a 20 mesh size is coarse, and a 60 mesh is fine. Sand may also be used to open out the clay, but if it is collected from places such as the beach or a builders' yard it must be tested before use to make sure that it does not contain iron pyrites (ferrous sulphide), which would blow up during firing. In fact many additions with which one is tempted to experiment must be approached with a certain amount of caution and common sense. Whilst it is a good thing to have an open experimental mind, some thought as to the temperature to which the piece will be subjected during the firing will save a great deal of time and frustration, to say nothing of possible harm to other pieces of work in the same kiln, and possibly even to the kiln itself, which can be damaged if foreign bodies used as 'experiments' cause a piece to explode.

Grog can be made out of many things. Already-fired clay such as firebrick, red-bricks and unglazed pottery, all ground up very small, can be used. Or it can be made by pounding up pieces of unfired clay, and then firing them in an unglazed container. A red-clay grog made in this way will give a good colour to a paler clay. Generally the grog should not be of a firing temperature that is lower than that of the piece in which it is to be incorporated, because it will melt. Such lower-temperature grog may be used intentionally, however, to give interesting mottled effects, as happens when a red earthenware clay is used in a stoneware body, but it is wise to experiment in controlled conditions first.

Grog can be mixed with powdered clay before it is reconstituted with water, or it may be sprinkled over sliced-open lumps of clay and then wedged in. A common practice is to sprinkle grog over the surface of the work-bench and then to wedge the clay on top of it so that the grog is gathered up into it.

If the grog has been incorporated in the piece primarily for the qualities of colour and texture which it imparts to the surface, it must be remembered that it will remain hidden inside the clay, and so give neither of these qualities, unless it is purposely exposed before firing. Scraping the surface is one way of exposing the grog. It also creates little pits and scratch marks, which can give an interesting texture to the surface. I find it best not to scrape the surface when it is very dry, because the little pieces of grog may be flicked out of the clay and fly up into the eyes. Sponging the surface will also expose the rough grog by removing the thin coating of clay which masks and covers it. Should the grog have been put into the clay for its 'opening' qualities and not for its texture, and a smooth surface be needed, then burnishing will satisfactorily tighten and smooth the work. For this I use the back of a metal spoon, but many different tools may be improvised—as will be explained in the section on African hand-building.

There are many ways of using these coloured and grogged clays creatively, once they have been made. When using them for effects similar to the banded patterning of pebbles and rocks, which first led to my explorations in this field, I needed the clearest division of the two colours which I could achieve. I therefore decided that inlay was the best method of introducing these coloured clays into the main body of the pebble forms.

Inlay

Inlaying gives as clearly defined a line as possible. The tools selected for making the grooves into which the clay inlay will be set are chosen according to the nature and condition of the clay. If the clay is smooth and leather-hard I have found that the most useful tools for cutting the grooves are wire modelling tools. These are available with a wide range of differently sized and shaped, rounded or angular, wire ends, and they make a very clean cut of an even depth. If the clay into which the inlay is to be put is either a heavily grogged one or has dried out too much for easy cutting something stronger than the wire tools will be needed. I find that lino-cutting tools serve the purpose very well, or pieces of specially cut and sharpened bamboo.

When all the grooves have been cut I lay in rolled-out strips of very soft clay. A thick slip may be used equally effectively. Whether the inlay is slip or plastic clay, the whole piece, pot and inlay, must be thoroughly dried out before cleaning up the surface. If not, the inlaid strip may well peel out when the surface is scraped clean. To make a thorough job the clay or slip will have been pushed or brushed into place without bothering too much about whether it spreads out on to the clay of the areas surrounding the grooves, so that a fair amount of tidying up is an inevitable part of the process. Actually this cleaning up is a very pleasant part of the work, because as the precise lines of inlay are revealed they look much better and crisper than one anticipates they will whilst waiting for the messy-looking surface to dry out.

Having found ways of making coiled pots based on simple banded pebbles, I started to think about interpreting another feature which I had frequently noticed occurring in pebbles and rocks. This was that the bands of different colours which run through them are often of a softer substance than the main part of the rock or pebble, and that this softer part becomes worn away into a pattern of deep hollows and struts by the action of wind and water, leaving its harder matrix relatively untouched. I began by including the coloured bands as separate coils while building up the walls of the pot. Sometimes as a variation on the horizontal banding I turned the coiled form on its side so that the coloured band ran from top to bottom of the form. To achieve an

The crystalline bands in the rock TOP *have been partially eroded, leaving the harder matrix merely softened in form. In the 'Eroded Form', unglazed stoneware, 1280°C* ABOVE, *oxided clays have been used for colour on the two hemispheres, and the central band is carved out to resemble natural erosion. 6½ inches high, 1964.*

eroded effect the differently coloured band was carved out in the leather-hard stage. Round-ended lino-cutting tools were used to make the initial opening through the clay wall. This small hole could then be enlarged and its shape varied by working on it with a long narrow knife or, for the finer work, with a needle. I found that the inclusion of grog in the main form gave a pleasant granite-like look, but I had to omit it from the carved section because it tended to make small holes and lumps which detracted from the clarity of the pierced work. I have not found that leaving grog out of a small section of the form makes any difference to the welding together or shrinkage of the two clays during the firing.

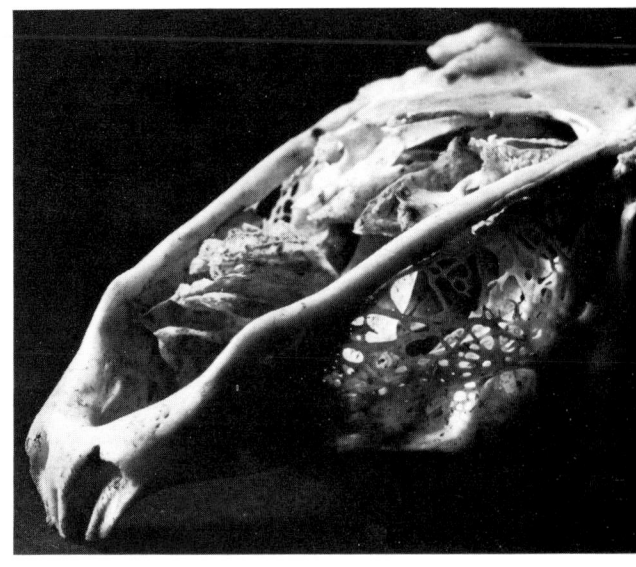

An eroded animal skull LEFT shows a filigree of three-dimensional form. In the deeply eroded stoneware 'Bone Form' below it the top was coiled with a very thick top section, and then carved at the leather-hard stage into layers of overlapping struts. Ash glazed, 1290°C, 6½ inches diameter, 1963.

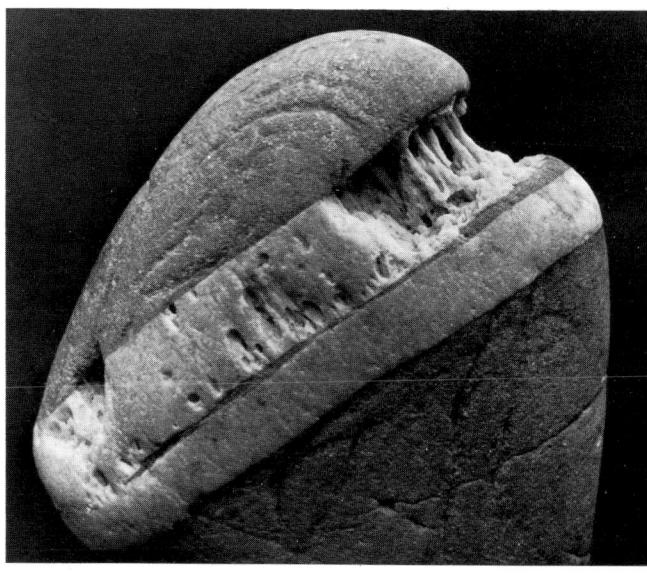

Another interesting variation was to include a band which was much thicker in section, probably twice as thick, as the main coiled form. This could then be carved out in depth, giving overlapping layers of strut-like supports, similar to those found in skeletal forms. There were no drying out or firing problems, probably because the carving had reduced the weight and thickness of the added

Different-coloured minerals appear within the eroded parts of the rock ABOVE. In 'Eroded Boulder' BELOW, unglazed stoneware, oxidized, 1280°C, a complete sphere was coiled and the central band deeply inlayed with oxided clay. This was then carved and pierced, and sculptured sections in the plain body clay made to protrude. 14 inches diameter, 1965.

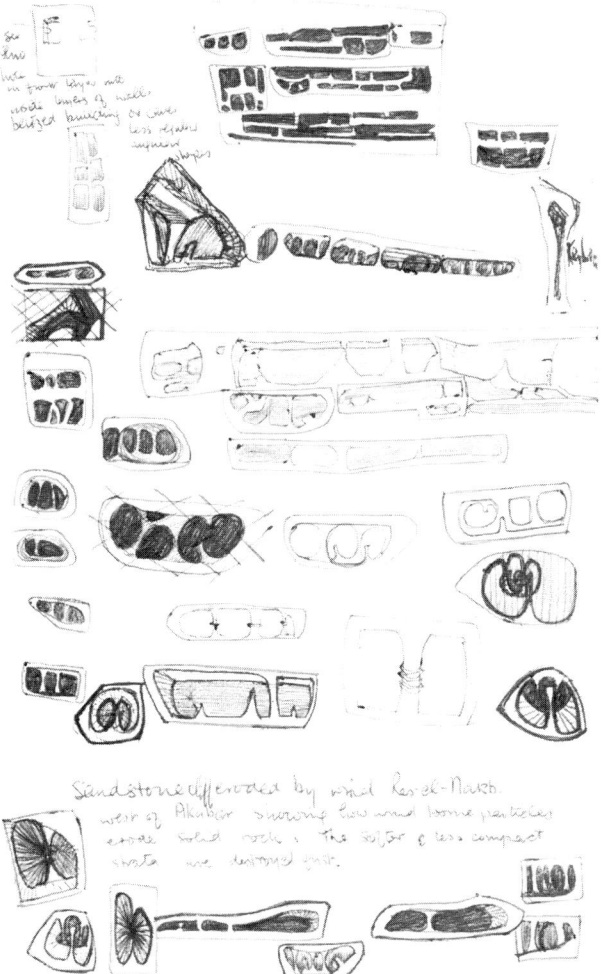

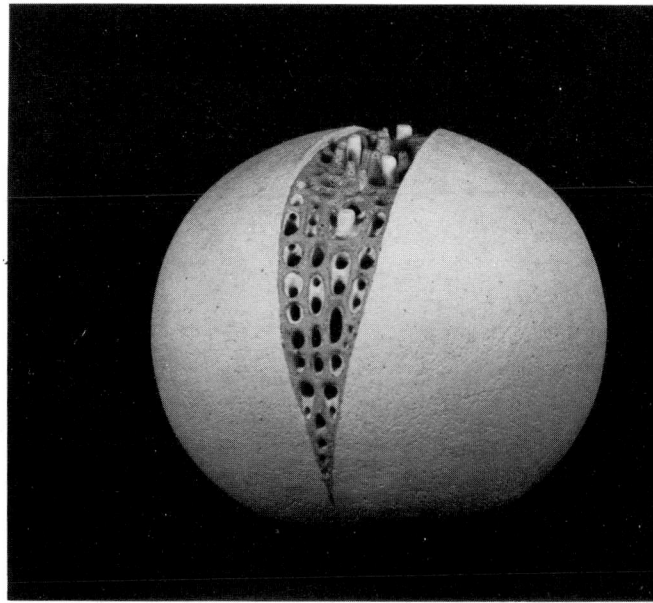

section, so that the 'eroded' area and the main walls were of more or less the same thickness throughout. It is in these carved 'eroded' pieces that the virtues of colouring the clays right through are seen to great advantage. However deeply the piece is carved, however undercut and complex, a differently coloured area will not be revealed, so that there is a convincing completeness of form and pattern.

Another way of using a combination of coloured clays is to weld together two or three different layers of clay, one on top of the other, and then to use this layered sandwich for carving into, in much the same way that a cameo is carved by exposing the different coloured layers of a shell or stone. The carving is done either in the leather-hard clay, or in the completely dry unfired clay, using it as though it were a piece of soft banded stone. This is not the same technique as that used for the familiar Wedgwood cameos. They are made by the technique of sprigging. For this a small piece of relief decoration in a contrasting coloured clay is made separately in a mould and then joined to the surface of a pot.

Inlays or appliqués may be added to pinched forms as they are built up. Coloured blobs, strips, and roughly torn off pieces of coloured clays are laid over the partly pinched-out main form. This should still be damp enough to be added to easily. These additions are then pinched in with the main form as the work progresses. This is a method in which results are only partly controllable and pre-dictable, unlike the true inlay technique, which gives very clear cut edges, prede-termined lines and areas of colour. With this pinched-in inlayed appliqué the results have something of the surprise of an ink-blob picture about them. Sometimes they are surprisingly good, sometimes not very pleas-ing.

There is another method of 'inlay' which I have not tried myself yet, but which I would like to mention because it sounds intriguing. It is described by Père d'Entrocolles in his letters which he sent back from China in 1712. He

1 **Pod Form** Porcelain, pinched, pierced and carved. Oxides painted under glaze, oxidized fired at 1300°C. $7\frac{1}{2}$ in. × 6 in.

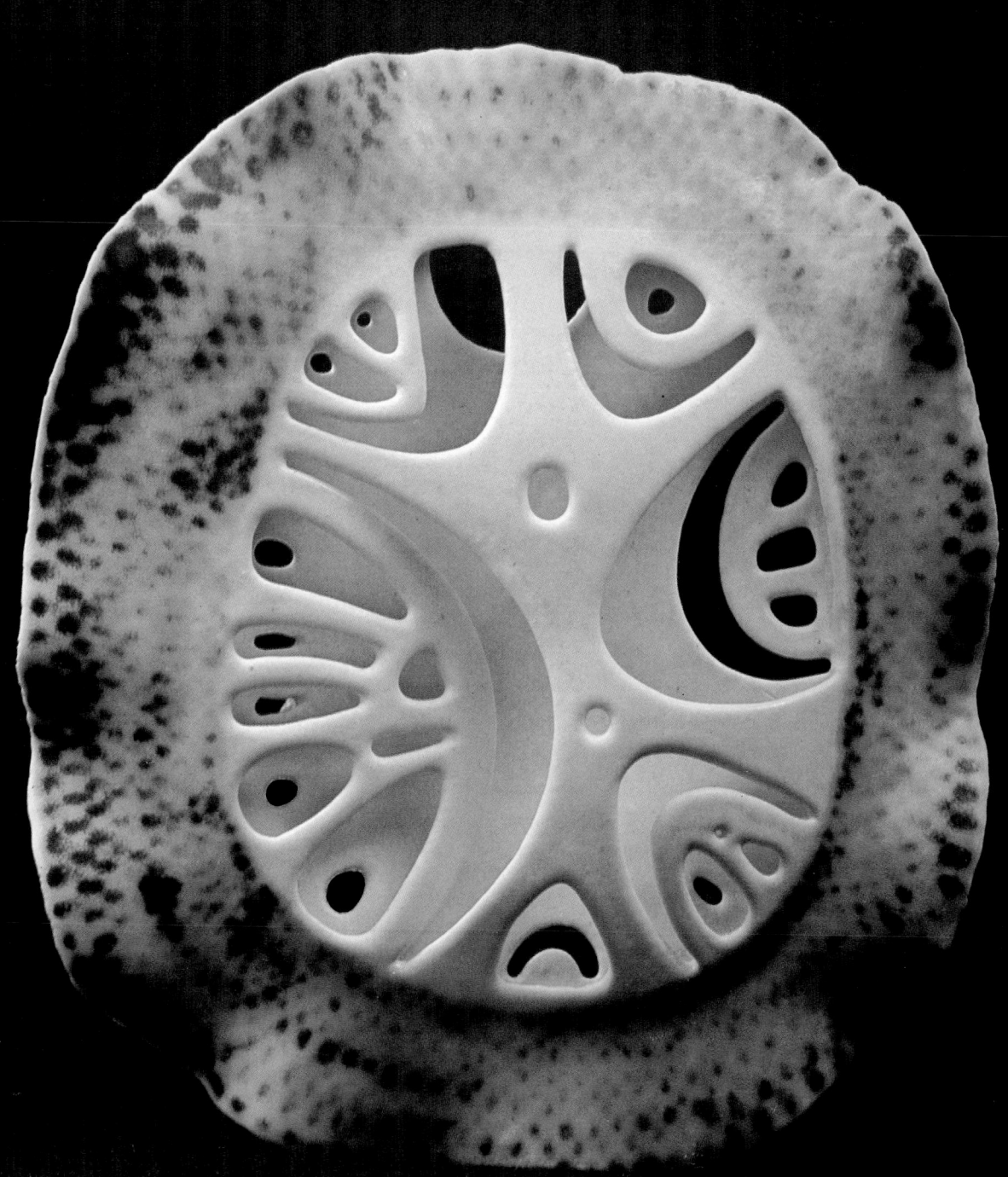

2 Convoluted Bowl Porcelain, pinch-built form with matt white glaze. Oxidized fired at 1300°C. 6 in. × 4 in.

3 Tree-edged Bowl Porcelain, pinch-built bowl with the rim pierced and carved. Crackle glaze, oxidized fired at 1300°C. $5\frac{1}{2}$ in. × $5\frac{1}{2}$ in.

4 Dappled Form
Porcelain, oxides used
under the glaze to
resemble a leopard's
camouflage coloration, or
the dappled cowrie
Cypraea Tigris **5**, below.
Oxidized fired at 1300°C.
8 in. × 6 in.

facing page:
6 Pink Flushed Bowl
Porcelain. Conically
shaped pinched bowl
with black tips. Oxidized
fired at 1300°C.
$5\frac{1}{2}$ in. × 4 in.

7 Sliced Agate Porcelain, pinched form contrasting
highly translucent uncoloured areas with less
translucent coloured areas, the total effect being similar
to the patterning found on sliced semi-precious stones.
Oxidized fired at 1300°C. 4½ in. × 4½ in.

8 Eden Apple Porcelain, pinched form with modelled
and carved interior. Oxides painted under glaze,
oxidized fired at 1300°C. 4 in. × 4 in.

says that the Chinese had themselves lost the secret of the technique at the time of his writing.

> They once knew the art of painting on the sides of porcelain pieces fishes or other animals that could only be seen when the piece was filled with some liquid. They call this kind of porcelain 'azure put in the press' because of the position in which the blue colour is placed. For this method the porcelain must be very thin; when it is dry they put the colour rather plentifully, not on the outside of the piece as is their usual custom, but on the inside. They generally painted fishes, as if they were more suitable to be revealed when the cup was filled with water. When the colour had dried, they put a thin layer of dilute slip upon it. This layer pressed the blue between the two sheets of clay. When the layer was dry they put the glaze inside the porcelain piece, and some time afterwards they put it on the mould on the wheel. As it had been thickened from the inside they pared it down on the outside without going as far as the colour, and after they dipped the outside of the porcelain piece in the glaze, and, all being dry, it was fired in the ordinary way. This was exceedingly delicate work.[7]

What sensitivity this suggests both in the potter exploiting the translucency of his material, and in Père d'Entrocolles' appreciation of the careful stages of painstaking craftsmanship needed in order to express the poetic idea of the hidden painted fishes, which 'were more suitable to be revealed when the cup was filled with water'.

Neriage (clay mosaic)

An ancient way of making ceramics which are patterned in the clay itself is to build the form in coloured 'clay mosaics' by the method which is called 'neriage' by the Japanese. It

9 Space Ellipse Porcelain pinched form, painted with a symbolic landscape. Oxidized fired at 1300°C. 5 in. × 5 in.

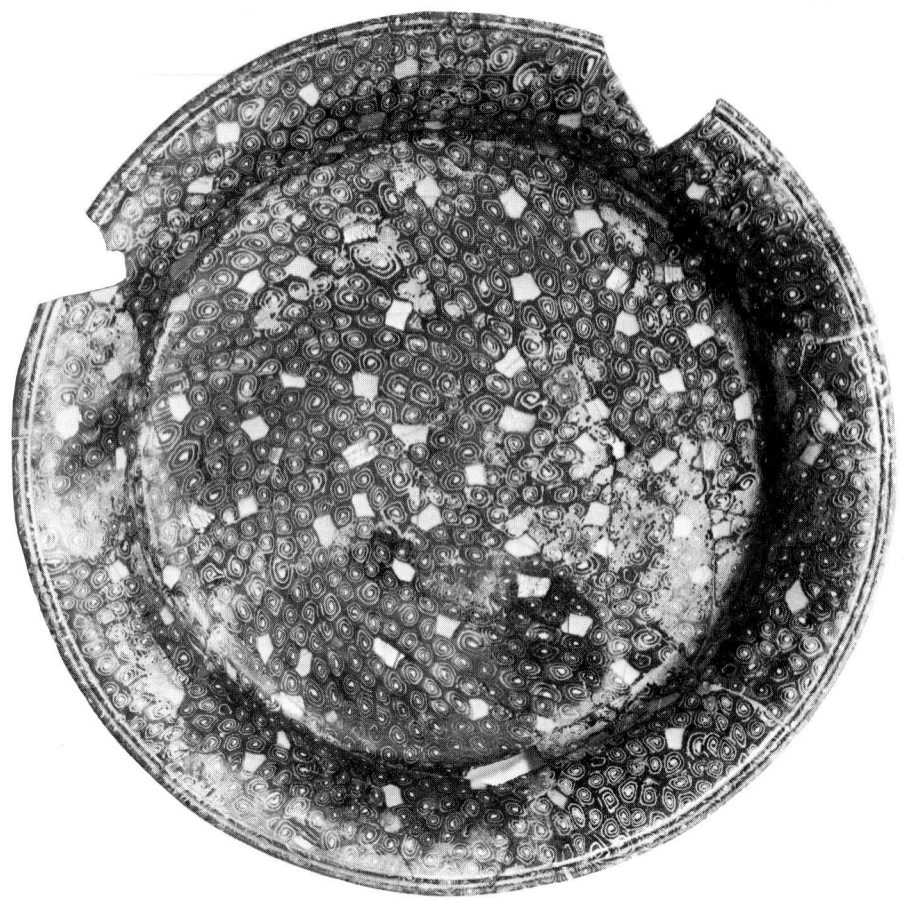

resembles millefiori glass, both in its technique and in its finished appearance.

The first step is to make rolls, or lengths of differently coloured clays, which are then laminated closely together by pressure. These multicoloured ropes of clay are then cut into small discs, or sections, in which the same pattern is repeated, like the lettering through Blackpool rock. These marbled sections are then laid inside a mould and eased and firmly pressed together into one piece. The shape grows by the addition of extra sections until it is completed. The sections may all be of the same pattern, or they may be taken from differently coloured coils, both multicoloured and single coloured, making very complex patterning possible. The finished result may be a fairly haphazard all-over pattern, or it can be a disciplined geometrically repeated one, which radiates like the patterns in a kaleidos-cope. Sometimes limited areas of coloured mosaic may be built up alongside single-coloured areas of clay. Whatever the pattern, the whole piece may either be left at the thickness of the sections themselves, or may be pinched out more finely after assembly. This handling will almost inevitably stretch and alter the patterning, and this may be anticipated and used as part of the intended effect. Finished pieces may be glazed or not, according to whether a dry or a glassy surface suits the work.

Marbled or agate ware

Yet another way of introducing colour, and decorating a piece in one process, is used for the production of agate ware. This is sometimes called *solid* marbled ware to distinguish it from the better known type of marbled ware in which only the surface covering of slip or glaze is marbled.

For agate or solid marbled ware two or more plastic clays of different colours are wedged together and formed into one homogeneous mass. There are various methods of doing this. The differently coloured clay strips may all be laid together and then either beaten until they form one solid mass, or unified by using the cut and slam method of wedging, or spirally wedged together. However the clays are combined, the less wedging that is done, the more widely spaced and clearly defined the contrasting colours will be; and the more the clays are wedged, the more evenly blended and diffused the coloured swirls will become.

When the clay has been prepared it is used to build pots by any of the usual hand-building methods. During the forming stage the fingers will inevitably make the surface smudged and blurred, and so cover up the true shapes and rhythms of the coloured patterns. This messy, undefined and somewhat disheartening stage occurs in agate ware pieces in the same way that it does in inlaid and appliquéd work. It is only after the final refining and scraping of the surface that the actual patterns of coloured clays are fully revealed. This is an exciting discovery each time.

As with other integrally coloured pots, agate ware may be glazed or not, according to the effect which is required. A glossy glaze will heighten the multicoloured look in much the same way that pebbles will show their patterned banding and colours more clearly when wet than when dry. A glaze of the more opaque variety will give a gentle blurred effect over the patterned clay.

In the eighteenth century agate ware was developed and used to a great extent, perhaps most beautifully by Thomas Whieldon (1719–95). But, as is generally found with all the infinite variety of possible styles of pottery making and decorating, the Chinese had explored agate ware long before. There are beautiful marbled bowls using these tech-

Agate bowl, 3½ inches diameter, 1973.

Marbled earthenware cup from China. T'ang Dynasty. Less than 2 inches high.

niques dating from as early as the T'ang Dynasty (AD 618–906).

I have found that the various methods I have described of colouring clay bodies and using them for inlay, neriage, appliqué and agate ware, all work equally well with either stoneware or porcelain clays. The only rule is that any one piece must only contain clays which reach maturity at the same temperature.

Glazing

The form of a glazed pot may be thought of as having an outside skin or covering which may be as fine, delicate and tight as the skin of a peach or the nacreous coating on a shell, or as coarse and pitted as orange peel. A glaze may seem to be part of the pot itself, to have grown there indivisibly from the main body, or it may lie over the form like a soft overlay of mossy cushioning on a rock, stopping short of the base, showing part of the clay of which the pot is formed and looking as though the thick roll of glaze could be peeled off or pulled further down. It may be as smooth and dense as glass, or it may proclaim, by small craters, its bubbling eruptions at white heat like molten rock down the side of a volcano. (This white-hot, slowly moving flow can actually be seen happening through the spy hole in the kiln if dark glasses are worn.)

Glazes serve practical ends by making pots more easily cleaned and impervious to liquids, but hand-builders are not generally making vessels for table-ware. These needs are better served by wheel-work. Most hand-builders are principally interested in glazes which add to the expressive qualities of the piece which is being made. Thus, dry, pitted, absorbent, crazed or crawling glazes may be used at will, so long as the effect appears to be intentional and in keeping with the work, and not a mere failure of skill.

Glaze-making can be a mathematician's delight or a chemist's challenge, but those of us who are naturally drawn to making pots as simply as possible by hand are most likely to want to make glazes for ourselves which are essentially uncomplicated, at least to start with. So it seems suitable to explore the sorts of glazes which were made by the earliest potters, who depended on experience and observation, creating the most beautiful glazes without using chemistry or theory.

It is suggested that the first glazes may have been the result of a chance occurrence, that some of the woodash used in a firing may have settled on the shoulders of the pots and left a deposit of glaze which was noted by the potter. He may then have sprinkled or rubbed ash into his next batch of unfired pots on purpose to form this coating during the firing. Certainly woodash rubbed liberally on a raw pot can give a pleasant coating of glaze when fired to about 1260°C. This is particularly pleasing over an iron-bearing body, or over a bland body which has been given a wash of iron. I have frequently done this to get a mossy-looking surface on a pot fired in an electric kiln. For this I do not wash my ash at all, but merely sieve it roughly with a domestic flour-sieve to remove any nails or pieces of twig from the bonfire.

Another simple glazing method, which may also have been discovered by accident, is that of painting a high-firing clay body with clay of a lower melting point. Possibly a low-firing piece of pottery was placed by mistake into a high firing kiln, and the resultant glassy melted mass suggested applying this low-firing clay (made into a slip for easier application) over a more refractory body so as to give it a glassy and rich finish.

Some of the simply made glazes on Japanese tea-ware, in which the rocks of which the glazes are made are barely fused and only roughly ground, giving beautiful tactile finishes, are one place to look for inspiration. So are the glorious glazes of early Chinese ceramics. These early glazes were developed by empirical methods, and consisted mainly of stones, clays and ashes which were ground, washed, sieved and applied to pots and then fired at high temperatures. For example, some of the most beautiful milky white glazes are simply pulverized feldspar fired on the pot at temperatures of between 1200°C and 1300°C.

Starting with this simple single material, feldspar, experiments can be done to give different effects by simple additions. For example, to make it flow more effectively a flux may be added. Whiting added as a flux in the proportion by dry weight of 15% whiting to 85% feldspar gives a good basic glaze at temperatures around 1250–1300°C. A combination of 60% feldspar with 20% whiting and 20% flint gives a glaze which is particularly suitable for porcelain; and so is the equally simple 25% feldspar, 25% quartz, 25% whiting and 25% china clay.

Woodash is material which can give beautiful glazes when used on its own and fired to stoneware temperatures. Each type of tree, plant, bush and grass gives an ash glaze with individual characteristics. The ash may be used as it is, straight from the bonfire or the wood-burning winter fire grate, or it may be sieved and washed several times and then dried and stored ready for use. With an electric kiln I find that one needs as much help as possible from accidental inclusions of 'impurities', and so I use mine unwashed and 'impure'. The ash may be rubbed generously on the slightly damp pot, or else mixed with water and either painted or poured on the raw or biscuited pot. If there is sufficient glaze the pot can be dipped into the glaze bucket or bowl. Again additions may be needed to make the ash behave better as a glaze. Either clay or stone, or both of these, may be added to the ash in varying proportions. For example:

china clay 50%
woodash 50%

ball clay 50%
woodash 50% (slip glaze for raw clay)

china stone 50%
woodash 50%

feldspar 50%
woodash 50%

These proportions may be varied by further trials of 10% either way to see what happens. For example:

clay 60%
woodash 40%

stone 70%
woodash 30%

And with both clay and stone:

woodash 50%
feldspar 25%
china clay 25%

These glazes will give different effects on different clay bodies, such as iron-bearing or white-firing ones, and the biggest difference will be in the firing atmosphere. Completely different effects will be seen with the same glazes in reduction and oxidizing atmospheres.

Oxides such as iron, cobalt, manganese and copper may all be brushed on, dabbed on with a sponge, sprayed on or painted on under the glaze to give further variations. Double dipping and wax resist add further to the range.

Another single glaze material is clay. This alone can make a glaze if taken to high enough temperatures. A clay which fuses at a relatively low temperature may be used as a glaze over a more refractory, high-firing clay. Common red clay, for example, will give a rich deeply coloured glaze on stoneware bodies. The fusion point of clays may be lowered further by adding a flux such as ash or feldspar, or both together. An effective glaze for porcelain may be made with the porcelain clay itself fluxed with limestone or ash.

Stoneware glazes may be used as porcelain glazes provided that they will fire satisfactorily at the high temperatures required for vitrifying porcelain bodies, that is around 1300°C. But as translucency is one of the main delights of porcelain, most potters prefer to use white, lightly coloured or translucent glazes rather than cover the delicate walls with a heavy or deeply coloured glaze. There is, however, no set rule about this; it depends on the characteristics of the material which one wants to capture and enhance. There is a rich, dense and mysterious quality about thickly potted and opaquely glazed porcelain. It is quite different in quality from stoneware, even when the same glaze is used.

Starting to make glazes in this way gives confidence, and may give such lovely and varied results on hand-built pots that no need will be felt for experimentation with more complex glaze formulae. If the glaze-bug does bite, however, there are a vast number of excellent and thorough books covering all aspects of glaze-making, with enough recipes and formulae to provide a lifetime's work in this field.

It should be said that the results from one potter's glaze recipes rarely turn out the same on another's work. There are so many variables that complete predictability is unattainable. There are the effects of different clay bodies, differing firing atmospheres and cycles, variations in the thickness of the pot walls and in the temperature to which the biscuit has been taken. If the pot has had a low biscuit firing it will naturally absorb more glaze than it will if it has been fired to a less porous state at a higher temperature.

There are various methods of glaze application. The glaze may be painted on, as is often done with raw glazed pots which are too fragile to be dipped in glaze, and which may distort if the glaze is poured on. Or it may be poured over the pot, especially if it is large and difficult to handle. For this the pot is ledged over the glaze bucket, or some other container, supported on two sticks or rods laid across the top of the bucket. The glaze is then poured around the walls of the pot, trying not to double glaze where the circle is completed (unless this effect is a feature of the design). Glazes may also be sprayed on. For small amounts this can be done with an atomizer spray, but this method usually requires the expensive equipment of spray gun, spray booth and compressor. But the simplest of all methods of glazing is dipping. First of all there must, of course, be a sufficient quantity of glaze to allow complete immersion of the pot.

Dipping the pot into the glaze and allowing the excess to run off often gives irregularities and drips, which will show on the fired surface as slight variations of colour. These can enhance the surface of hand-built forms. If a porcelain piece with very thin walls is being dipped I have found that this is best done as swiftly as possible, so as to allow only a very thin coating of glaze to adhere, otherwise it will flake off as it dries. With heavier-walled pieces the glazing may be done more slowly, and double-dipping is possible. This gives a deeper and richer glaze when both dippings are in the same glaze. Experiments with double-dipping in different glazes can be very effective and produce surprising results.

As I have said, there are very many books on the subject of glazing, and fully comprehensive sections within other books which deal with all aspects of pottery making. I would suggest to start with the very easy-to-follow section by Lynne Reeve in Michael Casson's book *The Craft of the Potter*, and many others, listed in the bibliography.

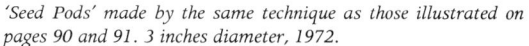

'Seed Pods' made by the same technique as those illustrated on pages 90 and 91. 3 inches diameter, 1972.

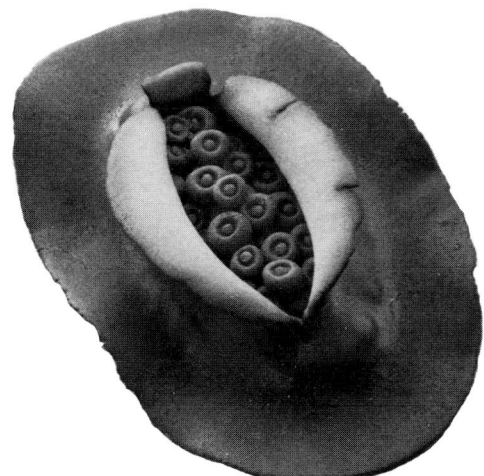

'El Pensador', a pottery jar representing a seated human figure from Colima, Mexico. 8½ inches high.

The tradition of hand-building

When making a pot by the simple method of using just the hands and the clay, it is possible to experience a very real link through time with man's earliest beginnings as a maker.

Clay was used during the Paleolithic era for making models of human beings and animals, but these were not fired but were just left to dry out naturally. Later, in Neolithic times, unfired clay was used for building up the walls and floors of houses. These were carefully made from layers of clay and were finally covered with red slip and then polished to a high finish. Bricks were also produced either by hand modelling or in moulds and were left to bake hard in the sun. These were used for building, with mud serving as a mortar.

During the last Ice Age, man had been making and using fire in his caves. But we do not know for certain when fire was first purposefully used to harden clay, to change it from a plastic material into a rigid and permanent one, and so to make pottery. It is sometimes suggested that the first pottery was made as the result of an accident, that a woven basket which had been lined with clay so as to stop things falling through the holes in the basket work, accidentally fell into a fire, and that when it was taken out later, the woven basket had burned away leaving a fired pot.

Another suggestion is based on the discovery of the shallow clay-lined pits in the floors of houses on Neolithic sites at places such as Jericho. These small pits are presumed to have been used as cooking places. It has been surmised that the fire-hardened clay lining, which would form a fixed basin inside these hollows gave people the idea of intentionally forming and firing bowls for other uses.

But however the discovery did come about, it was finally realized that, with the use of sufficient heat, the very nature of clay could be permanently altered from a soft flexible material into one of permanent hardness, in whatever shape man had given it. This seems to have occurred during, or possibly even before, the sixth millenium BC in the Middle East. Certainly by 5500 BC pottery was being produced in many villages in the Iranian Plateau, Syria and Palestine. It was first made in Egypt by the end of the fifth millenium, and in China at around 3000 BC.

All of these early pots were made without the potter's wheel, by methods of pinching and coiling which are essentially the same as those still being used today, both by potters who are continuing an unbroken tradition of hand-building, and by some of us who have made a deliberate choice of this way of working, finding it more sympathetic to a certain style of work and way of thinking.

The potter's wheel was not introduced everywhere at the same time, and hand-building continued as the principal method of making pottery in many parts of the world long after the wheel was invented. For instance, the wheel was unknown in pre-Columbian America, and all the magnificent pottery of the early civilizations of North and South and Central America was made by hand-building methods.

Hand-building has continued as the principal method of producing pottery in many technologically undeveloped parts of the world, but it is primarily in Africa that it has survived as a living tradition unbroken since earliest times. In many parts of the African continent, village potters are still forming pots quite naturally without the wheel and firing them without a kiln. The tradition is rich and varied and many of the specially notable qualities of the pots stem from the fact that they are hand-built. The character of hand-built pottery and the kinds of attitudes to work that it develops are nowhere better displayed than in Africa.

African women potters

Although the tools, materials and methods used by African potters are so simple, the production of such beautiful pottery must have been perfected by much painstaking trial and error over a long period of time, and the resulting knowledge passed down from one generation to the next, usually from mother to daughter, only very occasionally from father to son.

Making pottery by hand-building is usually considered, in Africa, to be a woman's activity, and little girls begin to learn the craft early, sometimes even as young as four or five years old, from their mothers or a female relative. The woman potter often makes her pots just for her own use within her own household. Often each woman in a village will make pots as a natural part of her many

activities. This she will do usually out of doors, either alone or else working in the company of a group of other women. Then all the pottery which has been made is fired together in a communal bonfire, everyone joining in with this. If she has made a few extra pots for sale at the local crossroads or market she will most probably carry them there balanced on her head, or possibly hanging in woven rope bags on the ends of a pole over her shoulders, in the same way that she will take the extra vegetables which she has grown. This rather casual attitude to their craft, fitting it in with the other household tasks, seems to be a fairly general one amongst the women potters of Africa, working within their own homes and villages. But there are some villages and larger centres, particularly those blessed with rich clay deposits, where all the women have become so skilful at making pottery that their finely made wares are well known throughout the surrounding countryside and are sought after by customers for miles around. Traders often come to these villages to buy on the spot. This happens, for example, with the Bamessi women potters: 'known throughout the grasslands as the most skilled workers in clay, Bamessi women potters have a virtual monopoly on the production of ceramics within the interior of the Cameroon.'[8] It is very interesting to see how an enthusiastic patronage of the potter's work is considered to have been important in forwarding the work of these craftswomen: 'The wide distribution of Bamessi pottery is due not only to a well-developed trade network, but also to the fact that Bamessi royal women gave many gifts of ceramic ware to the royal women of other chiefdoms. According to Gebauer, the head wife of Fon Njoya, who prized Bamessi ware above all others, had some fifty examples in her royal kitchen.'[9]

In the interior of Ghana and the Ivory Coast the ceramics of the Degha women potters are held in esteem. They live mainly in the villages along the banks of the Black Volta River and its tributaries and control the finest clay beds

Nupe cooking pot, Nigeria. Dark chestnut pot with incised patterning and burnished areas, 14 inches high.

A dark brown bowl from Inyi, made by Nwayieme, has the 'carved' appearance seen on other Ibo pottery. 7 inches high.

in the region. Every able-bodied Degha woman is a potter and they are able to produce about 400 pots each month in a centre such as Bondakele. Even in the smallest village about 150 pots may be fired monthly in a communal bonfire firing. These finely made pots are known, sought after and sold, not only to local people at the nearest market, but also taken by trucks up to 100 miles away for distribution and sale in distant markets. Besides making the pots, the women are also responsible for this widespread distribution of their wares.[10]

The Bamessi and Degha potters each form a sort of pottery-making community in the villages where they live, and large quantities of work are made for sale by all the women, using the unchanged traditional methods of hand-building and bonfire firing.

Rather different from this large scale production, there are also some African women who become known for their own personal and highly individual work. They may even 'sign' it with patterns which constitute a potter's individual trademark, and they often express an intense dislike of having their work copied by other potters. As Sylvia Leith-Ross says: 'One never feels they [the women potters] wish to dominate their material but rather cooperate with it. On the other hand, being individualists, they seldom resist some little twist or flourish which proclaims, "This is *my* pot. *I* made it." Hence the amazing variety of forms and patterns.'[11]

With this specialization and concentration by individual potters which encourages a great diversity of shapes and decorations, there also grows an increased expertise in making, and the potters become well known for their outstanding work. For example, an extremely beautiful bowl, which is in the Pottery Museum at Jos in Nigeria, was 'bought from Nwayieme, Inyi's best potter, who had used unmixed clay and the coil method. For decorating she used only the small 'comb', small pointed sticks, a pebble for polishing, and a wooden spatula.[12]

Methods of forming the pots

Whether just a few pots are casually made for personal everyday use, or a great many are produced by a village which is skilled in pottery making to be sold at the local market or further afield, or whether they are the individual work of a gifted potter and sought after or commissioned to be presented as special gifts to a bride or a new mother, all the pots will be made in basically the same simple

Igala water jar and storage vessel, Nigeria, decorated with white patterning on a red ground. A typical bridal gift. 22 inches high.

way. There are, however, intriguing variations of the basic methods which have evolved to suit local needs, and to make use of locally available materials.

The most obvious first necessity is the easy availability of a good plastic clay, and then there must be sufficient quantities of some sort of fuel for firing the finished pots. The simple tools which are used to shape, beat, refine, polish, decorate and colour the work are easily adapted from such things as pebbles, bark, leaves, and sticks, which are to be found everywhere. But, once again, these show interesting variations, and because they are found among or made from the natural products of the immediate environment, they reflect the way of life, the crops grown, the animals kept, and the nature of the surrounding area where the potters work.

The clay is usually dug by the potters themselves, probably from the nearby river bank, and carried back to their villages to be prepared for use. If it is a very good clay nothing further need be done to it. If not, it may have to be tempered by mixing in various additives. Such things as sand, finely ground pieces of broken pottery, finely weathered granite dust, or pulverized shells are the sort of additions which are made. They are pounded together with the clay in a mortar or on the ground, extra water being added if necessary, and when the ingredients are well blended together it is all kneaded to a good plasticity on a slab of wood, a stone, or just on the ground.

To work on the pot the potter may sit in front of it either directly on the ground or on a small seat of some sort. The pot may be rested between the thighs or knees, or when being burnished, scraped or decorated, it may be rested on the instep of a foot bent up to support it. The making of pottery by the women is all done with such natural ease that, for instance, there may be a baby suckling on the mother's lap whilst she is working on a pot placed on the ground beside the baby.

When the potter prefers to work from a

The pictures alongside illustrate pottery-making at Kigali, in Ruanda. There is division of labour. Half-made pots are seen ABOVE, *with the shape-maker on the right and the decorator on the left. A small piece of fired broken pottery is used to support the bottom of the pot which is being coiled up. This saucer-shaped support is rested in a small depression in the dusty ground, which enables the potter to turn the pot around whilst it is being formed. The older woman* TOP RIGHT *makes the main form and then the younger woman, who is working with her, refines and decorates this. To finish the pot she first pats it all over with a piece of wood to remove any unevenness, and to make the walls dense. Then the damp clay is decorated by rolling a piece of stalk around the form, which gives a spiralling ridged texture. This is repeated on the wide rim,* BELOW RIGHT *and* FAR RIGHT.

119

standing position she may still leave the pot on the ground, and bend down to work on it, bending completely double from the hips as she does so. But often, so as to give an easy upright working position, the pot is raised on a stand to make it a convenient height. This stand is often adapted from whatever is found to be suitable around the village. It may be one of the mortars in which grain is pounded. These are often carved from a piece of tree-trunk. To use this mortar as a pottery turntable a ring of grass, twisted into a circle, is placed on it, and then a piece of calabash or potsherd is settled into this grass ring. This is basically the same as the method used by the women for carrying pots, resting on a ring of grass on the head. The pot will be started in the piece of calabash or potsherd, which serves at the same time as both a rest and a mould. Sometimes a large broken pot with the shoulder and top rim still intact will act as a stand with the potsherd or calabash resting in its mouth. These stands function as a modeller's turntable; they are in no way like a thrower's wheel. What they enable the potter to do is to turn the work around slowly as one would do in the hands, so that it can be seen from all sides. With large pots, however, the clay is often manipulated whilst the potter walks rhythmically around the pot.

The potter walks around the pot which she is finishing. It stands on a saucer-shaped support which is rested in the mouth of a broken pot, of which the shoulder, neck and rim are still intact. Similarly-improvised modelling turntables are frequently used to support the work at all stages, from the first roughly coiled and smeared clay walls to the carefully shaped and decorated finished vessel.

Bassa Nkwomo Water Jar, 14 inches high, Nigeria. Incised geometric patterns are contrasted with burnished areas.

Many of the pieces are made with rounded bases and almost spherical forms. Apart from their beauty there are good practical reasons for their being the shape they are. A round hollow shape is a very strong one, and is best able to withstand the rigours of the bonfire firing. And afterwards it will stand up well to being used for cooking over an open wood fire, both because of the round shape and because it is of low-fired, heavily grogged, unglazed clay. When full of water these very large pots can be moved without being lifted, by being gently rolled over inside the supporting cushion of grass or cloth, or in the depression in the ground in which they are rested, tipping out just the right amount of liquid with ease. In the areas where these pots are made and used there is no need for a flattened base, or base ring, because the pots will hardly ever have to stand on a flat surface. Instead they will be placed on rings of plaited grass or on pads of cloth, eased into the dust or sand on the ground, bedded into a wood fire, nestled into a niche on an uneven floor, hung

on the walls or ceilings of huts in slings or cords, or else piled up, base into rim, around the huts and living quarters, making fantastic storage columns of differently shaped and decorated pots.

The beautifully swelling, rounded, full and springing forms of these pots are achieved and maintained during the plastic working stages in a variety of ways. Sometimes a series is worked upon in sequence. Each partly finished pot is inverted and left to rest, so as to stiffen a little, whilst another is being formed. When the first base is stiff enough to carry the weight of extra clay without causing sagging, the partly made form is turned the right way up again, and more coils are added to the top edge.

Alternatively, and this seems to be a very favoured method, the base curve of the pot is started in, or over, a rest of some sort. This supporting mould is often the base of an otherwise broken or discarded pot, or half a calabash may be used to lay the clay in, or a rounded boulder shape may serve as a support to hang the clay over. These rounded shapes, which act as both a mould and a support to the soft clay, will usually first be dusted with something such as woodash so as to stop the sticky clay from clinging to them. The clay may then be moulded either over the outside, or else, if it is a hollow mould, on the inside of the supporting mould. The pot may be started simply by pushing a lump of plastic clay on to or into the support. This is then eased, patted or beaten to take the shape of the outside of the hump or the inside of the hollow. A corn cob is sometimes used as a tool for pressing the clay into the mould. Occasionally a basket is used as a mould, in which case the clay is left until it dries out and the basket is then removed.

Another way is for the potter to flatten a lump of clay into a disc shape. This may be done with the feet by stamping on it, or with the hands by patting it out between them. This flattened pancake of clay is then placed over the rounded form which is acting as the support, and patted or beaten on to it both to thin it out and to accommodate the clay to its shape. The uneven top edge of the clay is usually cut off to straighten it, and when the whole form is stiff enough not to flop, the small bowl shape is taken off the support, and the walls are built up to the desired shape.

The use of a mould support gives a certain similarity of size and shape to each of the pots. But, of course, after the base has been formed in this controlled manner the rest of the shape may be modelled freely.

After the curved base has been formed in the support, the pot will be continued by coil-building. The coils may be rolled between the hands, or pinched out of a lump. They may be long enough to have to be supported along the arm, or even spiralled right round the forearm if a very long piece is used. Very often the coils are not long at all, but short and fat, rather more lumps than coils, of about 6 inches in length. However long or short, fat or thin, they may be, they are all fed on to the top edge of the pot and then smeared together so that no joins show, and a tight unified wall is created.

Finishing the rim. This picture was taken in the village of Kwali.

The rims are often finished off with a wet rag, a leaf, or a piece of dampened animal skin. For the coiling up process the potter may sit or stand at the work. Sometimes the pot is still and the potter moves round it, feeding the clay on whilst walking. On the other hand the potter may be stationary and the pot may be moved as the work proceeds. The pot may be on the ground, still in the piece of calabash or potsherd, or standing on top of a piece of leaf to prevent it from sticking to the earth, or it may be worked on at waist height still standing on the improvised 'turntable' stand.

There is another method employed for making pots which occurs with surprising frequency, and which seemed rather strange and contrary to me when I first heard about it. That is that the pot may be built up entirely without a base! A piece which is formed like this is often started with two large thick doughnuts of clay. Sometimes this fat open circle of clay will be rested on a leaf on the ground, and sometimes in a saucer-shaped potsherd or calabash. The entire walls and

Making a pot by building the sides and top first, and the base last, photographed in Zambia. The clay, dug from the stream bed, was formed into two fat doughnuts. These were placed one on top of the other, and pinched and smoothed to form the walls LEFT. *Extra clay was added to form the rim* BELOW. *The surface was then decorated with stamped and rouletted patterns. After this the pot was turned to rest on its completely finished rim* RIGHT *and the bottom was gently closed in and smoothed over with a piece of gourd.*

neck, top and rim, will be formed and finished—even including any stamped rouletted decoration—before any bottom is built on to it! The only reason that I can think of for this is that—particularly with a thick walled piece made rather quickly out of wettish clay—if the base is modelled on and closed up last, and the pot is dried out on its firm rim, rather than standing on this newly made, rounded, and still very soft base, the curve of the base will then be in no danger of being flattened by the weight of the clay above it. Certainly this sad collapse of the full swelling form intended by its maker is something which most first-time coil-builders find happening to their work as it gets larger.

Even simpler is the method by which Ashanti women in Ghana make the entire pot from one lump of clay. This is done by hollowing out and dragging up the clay to form the walls as they walk around it, bent double, with the lump of clay placed on the ground in front of them. In Ashanti only the men are allowed to make any pottery in-

corporating anthropomorphic and zoomorphic decorations or forms, because it is believed that making such things could cause sterility in a woman by confusing her natural role as a childbearer with that of making images in clay.[13]

Another simple method of making the entire pot from a lump, but this time forming the walls downwards over a core rather than upwards from a hollow, was seen in a village in Cambodia. Here the lump of clay is placed on the top of a stout post, which is then spun around in the hands whilst the clay is patted

and drawn out downwards over this 'mould', so forming a thinly potted vessel.[14]

However the pot may have been formed, it has to be tidied up, and any unwanted bumps, roughnesses and excess clay will be scraped off both the inside and the outside. Often pieces of calabash or gourd are made into scrapers with varying curves. They are very like our metal kidneys, and have the same useful properties, as they are stiff enough to scrape off the excess clay, yet have the right amount of 'give' and flexibility to accommodate to the inner and outer curves of the pot without shaving it into facets, as easily happens if inflexible, straight-edged tools are used.

Sometimes the final form is achieved by beating the pot into shape. This method also gives extra strength to the pot by compressing and consolidating the clay particles. It can also give something of the effect of burnishing, and will deepen the colour somewhat, and impart a slight polish. The tools which are used for this beating-out process are such things as suitably shaped water-worn pebbles or stones, or a snail shell, a pad of dry clay which has been formed to the shape of a dumb-bell, or a round wooden beater which is rather like the small pestles for pounding up spices in mortars. Sometimes the beater will be dipped in dust or ashes to stop it from clinging to the clay as it is used, or the clay itself may be dusted every so often. A coil-built pot may be beaten either to refine its shape and to fatten out depressions, or to thin out the walls.

Sometimes, however, the entire pot may be formed by the process of beating it out, rather as a metal pot may be 'raised', using a depression in the ground or a mould as the former in which it is turned and fabricated. When this 'metalworking' technique is used it seems to be the men who are the potters, as with the Adarawa Hausa of Sokoto. In India, however, it is the women who do the beating. In order to make the large spherical pots which are used in India to carry water, a man throws a roughly made, thick, plant-pot-sized pot on a simple wheel, and then the woman takes over. With various-sized pads supporting the inner wall, the shape is 'raised', thinned and made spherical by rhythmically beating the outer wall with paddles. The neck and lip, formed and finished in the first stage of throwing, are left untouched while the walls are beaten to an incredible thinness, and the pot grows to a huge size, whilst it is turned round and round, very swiftly, in the hollow in the ground in which it is cradled. Ash from the fire is used to make the surface dry and smooth during the beating, so as to prevent creases forming. Patterns with combs are finally made on the outside, each region having its own particular pattern. Finally the pots are fired on their rims, where the weight and thickness of the throwing has been left unaltered.

A pot which has been formed without having been beaten into shape is often burnished to give it a finish. This will also give strength to the pot in the same way that beating will do, by compressing and consolidating the clay particles in the walls. The tools for doing this are often prized personal possessions, which may be handed down from mother to daughter. They are improvised from such things as water-worn pebbles, snail shells, pieces of wood, or skeins of threaded beads made from seeds. Often the burnishing is done after the pot has been treated with a

Burnishing the rounded base of a pot, Tatiko, Nigeria.

wash such as red ochre mixed in water, or a fine textured red-firing clay slip. These natural colour coatings are rubbed on to the surface of the pot with a rag, and then burnished with the pebble, shell, seed bundle, or whatever else is found to be effective. When finished, the pots have the satisfying appearance of well-polished brown leather, or of a well-rubbed conker from a chestnut tree. There are often tiny facets which catch the light and glitter, showing, very subtly, how the burnishing tool has been used.

Decoration

A particularly striking feature of so many African hand-built pots is the bold way in which they are carved, textured and decorated. From the purely practical point of view the ridges and bumps can act as hand-holds, and the frequently quite rough and deeply textured areas on the almost universally spherical forms can give a very useful grip to the surface, particularly when such slippery substances as oil are kept in them. Aesthetically speaking, it is very likely that those peoples used to the clear definitions of form given by strong sunlight and shadows by day, and firelight or moonlight as the main sources of light after dark, would respond very strongly to the definite planes and hollows of the boldly carved, grooved and textured pots. These raised and impressed patterns clothe the body of the pot most beautifully, and are very like the cicatrization marks with which some African peoples decorate themselves. They emphasize a form in the same way, passing around it and drawing attention to its curves and volumes, contrasting textured areas against smooth ones.

The tools which are used to make these decorations on the pots are adapted from pieces of local vegetation, either used just as they are found, or else shaped and carved to suit their purposes. Such things as plaited

Storage vessel from Ankwe, Central Nigeria. In addition to distinct ridges and roulette patterns, there is a snake about to swallow a frog encircling the shoulder of the pot. 14 inches high.

Ibo Water Jar, Nigeria, 14 inches high.

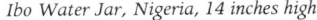

127

reeds and fibres, pieces of bark and rind, corn cobs and sticks are used, and frequently patterned roulettes are carved from wood. When the carved roulettes are used to impress the designs on the walls of the pot the roulette itself is sometimes dipped in water as the design is made or else the clay is dampened and the roulette gently pressed on. Sometimes, instead of the small carved wooden rollers, short lengths of a plaited reed or a fibre cord are used to give repeatable patterns. These have hard surfaces of little knobs and hollows, and look like pieces of solidified dressing-gown cord, or macramé. When they are rolled over, or pressed into the clay, they naturally give the reverse of the plaited patterns. A potter will often have a collection of these pattern-making tools for her own use.

A fascinating variation of this sort of all-over impressed patterning and texturing is used by the peoples of the Niger Congola Valley who, besides making pottery, produce mats, baskets and raffia bags. To texture their pots a depression in the ground is lined with a coarse net made of local string or coarsely woven matting, and the soft clay is lowered into this. Heavy stones are used inside the pot to press the clay firmly down into the net or mat-lined hollow, so that a clear impression of the textured patterning is left in the damp clay. The top of the pot is finished off with rouletted patterning.

Some of the decorations are made by carving out, rather than by pressing in. When this is done the incisions are made by cutting, because of the coarse nature of the clay which would give an unpleasantly ragged and broken-edged line if scratched. Some of these decorations are exceptionally fine, particularly those made at the village of Kwali.[15] Before sale the grooves are often filled in with guinea-corn flour to show that the pot is a new one which has not been used, much in the same way that we wrap a box in cellophane, or seal an unopened bottle of wine with wax.

Tiv brewing pot, Nigeria. The pattern on the lower half of this black pot was made by placing the base of the pot, whilst the clay was still soft, in a depression in the ground lined with a coarse net made of local string or a coarsely woven mat. Heavy stones were placed in the pot to weigh it down, thus obtaining a clear impression on the damp clay. 16 inches high.

RIGHT *New pots at Kwali*

128

Firing

Before they can be fired the pots have to be thoroughly dried out. Sometimes this is just allowed to happen naturally, and there appears to be no pre-heating of the ware, but usually the pots are thoroughly dried out and heated by such methods as being left overnight standing on their rims over the embers of a dying fire. Sometimes the fire is purposely built just to pre-heat the pottery. Michael Cardew describes how very large pots at Kwali are pre-heated by making a wood fire between three old pots or stones and, once the flames have died down, inverting the large dry pot over the glowing embers, its rim resting on the smaller pots or stones.[16] There it is left for an hour or two until it has become thoroughly warmed through. Then, whilst still hot, it is carefully placed, once again rim downwards, over a raft of the glowing embers of a second fire which has been especially made in the open. Carefully covered with sticks so that no part is left exposed, it is fired for about one and a half hours under the bonfire. In Benin, pots which have been dried in the sun for a few days are put on a bamboo rack which is supported on forked sticks two or three feet above the ground. Under this shelf, on a bed of fine sand, a fire is lit, and the pots are smoked for an hour. Then the heated pots are put on to this hot sand, and more bamboo sticks are stacked up all around them like a wigwam, and it is all burned for about an hour, using the bamboo sticks as fuel.[17]

Another way of pre-heating the pots before firing is to fill them with dry grasses which are then burned inside them. But, however the pots may be pre-heated, this must be done immediately before the proper firing. The pots must not be left around afterwards to get damp or they will burst all the more readily. The actual firing area may be surrounded by a circle of boulders, and it may itself be pre-heated with a small fire, but as firings are frequent this is not always necessary. A layer of potsherds may be placed on the ground before the first layer of fuel, and a raft is often built up to form a platform on which the dry pots are placed. Sometimes layer upon layer of alternating pots, brushwood and grasses are formed, and as the firing progresses the ashes help to cushion the pots which settle down from the top layers on to the bottom ones. Sometimes the pots may be piled up in a seemingly haphazard manner, or carefully arranged with the largest pots in the centre, and the smallest ones on the outer edges. They may be arranged to form a spiralling circle, like a Catherine Wheel, the largest pots in the centre, lying on their sides, abutting neck into base, and diminishing in size towards the smallest ones on the outer circumference.

At times one pot may be fired singly by an

LEFT *Preheating pots by burning grasses inside them.* RIGHT *and* BELOW *Selecting and arranging pots on the raft of sticks.*

individual, and sometimes hundreds are fired together in a communal firing. Everyone seems to join in and help with the stacking and gathering of the fuel. This fuel can be maize cobs, corn-stalks, dried dung from cows, sheep or goats, grasses, twigs or brushwood. There is a very satisfying and complete cycle of potting and agriculture practised by the Kofyar on the edge of the Jos Plateau. Here the women fire their pots in the depressions left between the ridges of guinea corn and millet after these have been harvested. Pieces of the guinea-corn stalk are also used in making the pots for smoothing over the inner surfaces and in finishing off the rims. The pottery is only made during the dry season, being fitted in with the rhythm of growing the crops.[18]

The common factor for all of the pots made by these simple traditional methods is the shortness of the time taken to fire them, and the lowness of the temperature reached. The actual flames last for a very short while, perhaps twenty minutes, but the fire then smoulders, and sometimes this smouldering is made to last for a longer time by adding wet grass or leaves, or by spraying water over the outside of the clamp. Extra fuel of some sort may be added to maintain the fire, but about two hours seems to be the maximum for any firing, and it may be as little as half an hour. The temperature which is usually reached is between 600°C and 700°C, which is the ideal temperature for the uses to which the wares are put. It produces a pot with great resistance to thermal shock, which will be needed when it is used for cooking over an open fire. Also, the considerable porosity of the walls, due to the low-temperature firing and the unglazed surfaces, has obvious advantages for use in a hot country when the vessel is to be used as a container for water, because the porous walls aid the cooling action of evaporation.

After the firing the pots may be left undisturbed in the bonfire until it all cools down, or they may be lifted out, on the end of long poles, while still red-hot, so that the surface can be sealed by various methods. One of the ways in which this is done is to immerse the red-hot pot in wet leaves, which then smoulder, driving the carbon right through the walls of the pots and sealing them completely. A favourite treatment is to prepare a liquor made from boiled-up bean pods, or from tree-bark, or local herbs or roots, and then either to dip the pot in the liquid or pour or splash it on the pot. The effect of this is to seal and strengthen the walls and give them a rich colour, which can even have the appearance of a glaze.

It is good to know that these most basic methods of pottery-making are still living and thriving as an unchanged craft tradition in very many places throughout the African continent. The advent of plastic and metal containers has not yet altered the situation very appreciably, because village pottery has so many advantages. It is very cheap and fits in well with the way of life of its users and makers. It is still the most obvious and best choice in most cases and, happily, shows little sign of being replaced or dying out yet.

ABOVE *Ibo ceremonial palm wine jar, from Nigeria, 6 inches high.* BELOW *Ibo kettle for palm wine. A dark brown pot with a fish-mouth spout, 5 inches high.*

5

Porcelain

As for pourcelain 'tis not made of plaster or egg shells beaten fine, but of a certain earth. ANON [19]

It is interesting to imagine the speculation about the nature of porcelain which preceded the statement alongside, made in 1683.

Translucent porcelain was first made by the Chinese during the T'ang Dynasty (AD 618–906) and it was not long before its particular qualities were recognized and sought after outside China. In AD 815 a merchant traveller from Islam, called Suleiman, wrote, 'The Chinese have a fine clay of which they make drinking vessels as fine as glass, one can see the liquid contained therein, though they be made of clay.'

Above all, it was the translucency of the porcelain vessels which was remarked upon by this observer eleven hundred years ago, and it is this same quality which is still a source of delight to lovers of porcelain today. The way in which the light passes through the clay walls is very beautiful, making them luminous and seemingly lit from within. Even a thick-walled piece has a halo of light on the thinner edges, and a visible depth to its substance like polished alabaster. It is very different from the dense impenetrability of stoneware clays, or the warm earthiness of earthenware pottery. But it is different also from glass, which light certainly passes through, but generally with a hard and glittering clarity as though through clear water or diamonds. It is more like the soft milkiness of light passing through semi-

Ting ware porcelain ewer, Chinese, Sung Dynasty, 6 inches high.

precious stones such as jade, or thin marble.

Certainly it must have seemed obvious to potters trying to find the secret of manufacturing a porcelain with the qualities so much admired in the Chinese pieces to think of adding glass to the clay so as to gain this translucent character. Indeed it appears that attempts to make a translucent porcelain by incorporating glass were made as early as the fifteenth century at one of the Venetian glass works. But it was in Florence, during the sixteenth century, that powdered glass, or glassy frit, was first used successfully with clay to give a type of porcelain. The work was carried out under the patronage of the Medici family, and so it is known as Medici porcelain. According to Vasari it was Buontalenti, a painter and sculptor, who was largely responsible for the first successful experiments. But only a very small amount of this Medici porcelain seems to have been made.

The next similar and successful experiments in porcelain-making, by once again incorporating a glassy frit with the clay, appear to have been in France in 1673, at Rouen and then at St Cloud. The characteristics of this porcelain, known as *pâte tendre* in France and as soft-paste, glassy or frit porcelain in England, are different from the 'true' hard-paste porcelain of the Chinese, which the makers were trying to emulate. But it does have great beauty in its own right. The use of the word 'soft' or 'tendre' does in fact describe, to some extent, the qualities of this material, though it is really a reference to the lower temperature needed for firing it. Soft-paste glassy porcelain is low fired at around 1100°C, with a second, even lower temperature for the glaze. Hard-paste porcelain is high fired, the temperature needed to bring about the necessary vitrification of the body and fusion of the glaze at one and the same time being from 1280°C, to as high as 1450°C for industrial porcelains. The frit or glass used for this glassy frit porcelain was painstakingly made. It is known from the accounts kept at Sèvres that it was composed there of sand, saltpetre, sea-salt, soda and alabaster, and that this frit was then ground together with the clay for three weeks, the proportion being two thirds frit to one third clay by weight. The clay which was used was a marl containing clay and lime. The mixture was not very plastic, and was fired at 1100°C.[20]

In England soft-paste, glassy or frit porcelain—made from pipe clay, sand from Alum Bay and glass— was first used at Chelsea and Bow at around 1744, and it was soon adopted at Derby and at Longton Hall in Staffordshire.

Soft-paste glassy porcelain is a beautiful material, and during the first half of the eighteenth century, both in England and France, its particular qualities were used with directness and charm, exploiting the soft sensuality of the white-glazed body, often with delicate, melting, diffused colours painted with a light and restrained touch. The pieces are indeed soft, tender and lovable. But, despite its undoubted merits and popularity, soft-paste glassy porcelain had a short life. It was found to have too many practical disadvantages. It was difficult to handle, it frequently slumped, distorted and even melted during the firing, and there was consequently a great deal of kiln wastage. Also, the low-fired soft glaze was easily scratched and stained, and the finished pots tended to crack if used to hold hot liquids—a great disadvantage when coffee and tea were the fashionably new drinks. So the search for a stronger and more stable porcelain was continued.

By 1770 a bone ash body had replaced the glassy porcelain in England, whereas by 1768 in France china clay and china stone (kaolin and petuntse), the main ingredients of Chinese porcelain, had been discovered at St Yrieix, near Limoges, and Sèvres had started to produce its hard paste porcelain. The hard paste was found to be more plastic, which suited the extravagant and grandiose style of work which was by then very much in demand, first by the courts, and, after the French Revolution of 1789, to satisfy the pompous Imperial taste of the Napoleonic period. Nevertheless, during the second half of the eighteenth century, both in France and in England, charming work of a light-hearted and playful kind continued to be made, using porcelain with sensitivity and restraint, and a feeling for its own particularly delicate nature. The tendency for much of the work to be what we would call 'sugary' is not really surprising when we realize that many of the pieces were intended to form the elaborately decorative centre pieces for banqueting tables, and were purposely made to replace those which had formerly been in sugar and icing!

Another factor which added to the increasingly elaborate and highly decorated tendency of much of the work in the second half of the century was that the potter, the person who actually formed the clay, did not usually decorate the pieces which he had made. The undecorated pots would be handed over to painters to be decorated, sometimes miles away from the place where they had been formed. These professional painters, with their often exquisite and painstaking work, as demanding as that of the miniaturist, would be more likely to think of the pot merely as a background to paint on, than to reflect on the form of the piece and the substance and nature of the plastic clay from which it had been made. So there was a break in continuity in the work. The tendency was for the body to be completely obscured by heavy decoration, and for the work to become rather heavily opulent and ostentatious as the century progressed. It is as though, having at last mastered the technicalities of porcelain making, ceramic artists were persuaded to go to every extreme to explore its decorative possibilities, partly no doubt to satisfy their own curiosity, but chiefly to please their rich clients, who would be trying to outdo and impress their neighbours with their collection of porcelain extravaganzas. Another factor which tended towards excessive over-elaboration, particularly in France with its Royal patronage, was that porcelain was treated as a rare and precious material, and a great deal of time and work would be expended on each item, because such high prices could be obtained for each piece. The finished porcelain pots were essentially for the use and embellishment of rich and ornate palaces, and were put into the same category as work in silver and precious stones. In fact pieces were often mounted in gold and silver, while silversmiths often became porcelain makers, porcelain replaced silver plate for fine table ware, and work in silver was often directly copied in porcelain, and was prized as highly.

By the end of the century hard paste had replaced the former *pâte tendre* throughout France, but the English manufacturers had, instead, adopted bone ash in their recipes to give strength to the body. There is a German recipe from 1649 giving oyster shells and burnt bones as ingredients for making porcelain, but what led to the first serious trials, a hundred years later in England, in which largish proportions of powdered calcined bones were added to the clay body, must be a matter of speculation.[21] It may even have been the verbal analogy of putting the firmness of bones into a weak body to strengthen it which started the train of thought. This can be the way in which the mind works. Often the solution to a problem is found through the bringing together of substances which look as though they ought to work from a purely visual or intuitive viewpoint. Certainly, in the search for the secret of strong translucent porcelain which could be formed with ease by the potter, imaginative jumps and hunches must often have been resorted to, sometimes with success, sometimes not. Think of the 'egg shells beaten fine' of the quotation at the beginning of the chapter. Maybe the undoubted visual similarity of cleanly bleached, delicate, polished pieces of bone to translucent white porcelain was noticed, and pondered upon, by a potter or a chemist who was searching around for the 'secret ingredient' of the much admired porcelain.

But whatever did lead to it, it was discovered, in the middle of the eighteenth century in England, that a proportion of up to 40 per cent of calcined bones, crushed and ground to a powder and added to the soft paste, did give a very durable and beautifully translucent porcelain. The sort of soft-paste bone porcelain which resulted from the addition of bone ash to the soft paste body, was found to be stronger than the previous recipes with the glass frit. It could be potted very thinly, and did not warp in the way that glassy porcelain had been found to do.

Soft-paste bone-ash porcelain was first made at Bow in about 1747, and was almost immediately adopted by other pottery manufacturers such as Chelsea, Lowestoft, Derby and Liverpool. Later, around 1800, Josiah Spode the second, combined the ingredients of hard-paste porcelain with bone ash, and so produced the type of bone porcelain, or bone china, which is still used today. A bone ash body is sometimes referred to as a phosphatic body because phosphoric acid is a constituent of bone ash.

At about the same time that the experiments with bone ash were first being conducted in England, another line of experimentation was being followed with the naturally occurring rock soapstone, or soaprock. This suggests by its visual appearance that it might well combine with clay to give a strong translucent porcelain. From its name it is easy to envisage what soapstone or soaprock looks and feels like: it is a smooth, light coloured, soapy or greasy-textured rock, composed mainly of talc. When powdered it is known as French chalk. It was discovered in Cornwall, and was first tried out as an addition to the porcelain body at Lund's factory in Bristol, and was found to give just the right qualities of strength which were being sought. The soaprock porcelain could be potted thinly, and with precision, and vessels made from it were able to hold hot liquids without cracking. The Bristol factory which first used it in 1750 was moved to Worcester in 1751, and Worcester continued to use the soaprock porcelain until around 1800, when it was replaced there by the new hard-paste bone porcelain. The proportions of soap-rock used in the body at Worcester were from 35–50 per cent. Soaprock was also used at Liverpool and Caughley, and there seem to have been some similar experiments at Derby, with a recipe brought by an employee of Worcester when he went to Derby to work for Duesbury. But it does not seem to have been taken up by the Derby works, who adopted the soft-paste bone ash formula when they bought up the Chelsea factory in 1770, and began to make pieces in the newly fashionable Neo-Classical style.

There was a great deal of money and prestige involved in the manufacture of porcelain during the eighteenth century, and any newly discovered methods for its manufacture, and of the materials used, were kept as closely guarded secrets. Nevertheless, each new discovery was quickly adopted by rival firms. Workmen often left one employer to sell what they knew to another; sometimes enticed away by the rival firms, sometimes moving there of their own free will in the hope of gaining substantial financial reward. This network of 'industrial spies' in the ceramic industry operated not only throughout England, but throughout Europe, and from Europe potters brought their own knowledge over to England as well. Besides this, factories copied each other's designs shamelessly, both in shape and decoration, in order to gain the market. They also, of course, inevitably copied the Chinese and Japanese porcelain which was shipped to Europe in such enormous quantities.

The growing market for Chinese porcelain can be gauged from the fact that in 1701 100,000 pieces were exported from Ching-tê-Chên, while sixteen years later, in 1717, two British ships alone were each instructed to buy 305,000 pieces. These must have found a ready market because, in 1721, four British ships were sent, and these brought back a total of 840,000 pieces. This is doubly amazing when one thinks how small the total population was at that time, and how very small a proportion of this number would be able to afford such expensive luxuries anyway. It gives an idea of the keenness of the market, and therefore of the pressure on potters and chemists to find a way of equalling and, if possible, supplanting these imports by discovering for themselves the secrets of porcelain manufacture, and the correct materials with which to work. Britain was not alone in importing the Chinese porcelain on such a grand scale. There were at one time thirteen trading posts belonging to the Dutch, French, Danes, Swedes and Americans. It must have been a hazardous undertaking to carry such a fragile and valuable cargo so far in sailing ships. The pieces were apparently packed in sago for the voyage.[22]

Very instrumental in spreading the knowledge of Chinese methods of porcelain manufacture in the eighteenth century was Père d'Entrocolles. He was a Jesuit priest who lived and worked in China for forty-three years, and who sent back letters to his native country of France in which he painstakingly described everything that he was able to observe about the making of porcelain. Amongst his flock of converts to Christianity were Chinese potters, and he obviously had free access to every part of the great porcelain town of Ching-tê-Chên, which he described as 'looking like a town on fire at night, so numerous were the lighted kilns'. There were three thousand wood-fired kilns in the city, and if they were all firing at once it must have been an awesome sight. His letters, written in 1712 and in 1722, were published in full a few years later. They were also included in du Halde's book *Description de l'Empire de la Chine* in Paris in 1735. Three English editions of this book appeared between 1738 and 1741, and for those interested in porcelain and its manufacture the carefully detailed letters of the Jesuit provided an invaluable fund of information.

William Cookworthy, 1705–80, a quaker apothecary of Plymouth, was familiar with the letters of Père d'Entrocolles, and during his many travels throughout Cornwall over a period of twenty years he was continually searching for, and experimenting with, various materials similar to those which the Jesuit had described as being necessary for making porcelain in the Chinese manner. He was helped in this by a local landowner, Thomas Pitt, later to become Lord Camelford, who gave Cookworthy financial assistance in his venture, and on whose land Cookworthy first discovered kaolin (china clay). Later he found the necessary feldspathic rock, the Cornish 'Growan Stone' (Cornish stone or china stone), the equivalent of the Chinese 'petuntse'. Now, with these two materials, true hard-paste porcelain could be made in England from English materials. He took out a patent for this hard paste in 1768 and, helped financially by Lord Camelford, opened a factory at Plymouth, which was moved to Bristol two years later. So it will be seen that by the year 1768 the materials for hard-paste porcelain had been found in both France at St Yrieix, and in England in Cornwall. But whereas the French adopted the hard paste, in England the generally preferred variety of porcelain continued to be that with the bone ash addition.

The styles of the emerging French and English porcelain manufacturers of the eighteenth century were influenced not only directly by the Chinese, but also by the hard-paste porcelain of Meissen in Germany, which had been established in 1710, and also, of course, by the imports from Japan, which had been producing porcelain since 1616. It was a captive Korean potter, Ri Sampei, who found the materials for making porcelain in Japan. He found them near Arita, which rapidly became a porcelain-making centre, exporting its wares to Europe in vast quantities from the nearby port of Imari.

The way in which the Germans were the first in Europe to find the much-sought-after secrets of porcelain manufacture, approximately fifty years before the rest of Europe, is a fascinating story. The quest to find a way of producing this expensive and valuable commodity seems largely to have been spurred on by the collecting mania of Augustus the Strong (1670–1733) King of Poland and the Elector of Saxony. So heavy a cost to the country's exchequer was his enthusiastic spending on his great collection of Chinese porcelain that China was referred to as 'the bleeding-bowl of Saxony'. To ease this situation Augustus's economic adviser, Ehrenfried Walther, Count von Tschirnhaus, a renowned physicist, was trying to discover the secrets of porcelain-making, and so cut down the imports by replacing them with pieces produced at home from local materials. He was also engaged in experiments with native rocks, minerals and earths, hoping, by subjecting them to very high temperatures, to turn them into precious and semi-precious stones. At the same time, near Meissen, a young alchemist, Johann Friedrich Böttger, was similarly attempting to turn base metals into gold, and after having failed to do this over a period of three years, his failure causing his imprisonment, he was released in order to work with von Tschirnhaus. In 1708, in the course of their experiments together, Böttger and von Tschirnhaus discovered how to make true hard-paste porcelain with materials which they had found in the neighbourhood of Meissen. In 1710, a factory for making porcelain was established at Meissen by Augustus, and it was an enormous success.

It is interesting to muse on the effect that patronage has on the style of an artist's and craftsman's work, whether it is that of the state, the accepted religion, or of an enthusiastic private collector. If the private collector is also an arbiter of fashion, as the ruler of a court so often has been, then his own personal taste may become the overwhelming style which the artist craftsmen of his time strive to satisfy. This certainly happened with Augustus of Saxony, as it did later with the patronage of the Sèvres factory by Louis XV and his favourite, Madame de Pompadour, who by their own luxurious lifestyle and pastoral daydreams promoted a fashion in porcelain which lingers even today.

Augustus, the prime motivator behind the early emergence and success of the German hard-paste porcelain of Meissen (sometimes loosely referred to as Dresden), certainly had tastes which seem to have led to a whole style of work both in his Meissen factory and in the many porcelain-making concerns which sprang up to copy its much sought after products. He not only collected porcelain with what he admitted himself was an avidity which amounted to a malady, but he also had a mania for collecting animals and birds, particularly rare ones, for his zoo and aviary. These two interests, in natural history and in porcelain, came together in his 'Japanese Palace', which he purchased in order to fill it with his existing collection of Chinese and Japanese porcelain, and with pieces made at his newly established factory of Meissen. The pieces which he ordered from this factory were porcelain models of lions, leopards, elephants, bears, monkeys, eagles, storks, parrots and cockatoos. These were made sometimes literally as large as life, as Augustus dreamed that they should be, by such artists as Kirchner and Kändler.

This passion for wildlife, allied to a passion for fine craftwork, is interestingly paralleled by another ruler in an entirely different environment and age. Of a ruler in ancient Mexico, it is recorded that, 'The king kept all species and varieties of birds, animals, reptiles and snakes which were brought to him from every province . . . and those which could not be obtained he caused to be depicted in gold and precious stones, likewise sea and freshwater fish. So no animal of the whole country was wanting here; they were either alive or figured in gold and gems.'[23]

Porcelain means many things to many people. It does not come from one clay which can be dug, complete and useable, but it is made up of at least two substances, which need to be very accurately and carefully blended, and then fired at a very high

White glazed porcelain figure of a goat, 22 inches high. Modelled by J. J. Kaendler for the Japanese Palace at Dresden of Augustus the Strong. Meissen, about 1732.

temperature. It is a word which has no exact meaning, but means whatever potters and collectors have decided are the qualities which a piece must have before it may be called porcelain. But these qualities have varied from one culture to the next, with a varying scale of importance, and a piece may not possess all of the necessary qualifications, and still be beautiful porcelain. In fact there is not one porcelain, but many types, and even now a hornet's nest may be stirred up by calling a piece 'porcelain' when it does not conform, in one aspect, to one understanding of the word.

Part of the confusion has, I suspect, arisen from the use of the word 'true' to describe one species of porcelain, and 'artificial' for the others. The model which has been taken as 'true porcelain' was the Chinese hard-paste porcelain. Thus many ceramics possessing beautiful porcellaneous qualities, but not made with only the two materials kaolin and petuntse (thought to be used with no additions by the ancient Chinese) are often called 'artificial porcelains'.

These two words 'true' and 'artificial' are very emotive and even moral words, and I feel have caused confusion amongst some potters with their overtones of 'real' and 'honest' in the case of true porcelain, and 'false' or 'feigned' in the case of artificial porcelain. In fact sometimes true porcelain is known as 'natural', as though the 'artificial' is in some way 'unnatural', whereas they both, of course, are made up of various proportions of naturally occurring rocks, clays and minerals, and sometimes bones, which are all equally natural products of the natural world, though neither the 'true' nor the 'artificial' porcelain can occur without the help and labour of man.

The rocks which the Chinese used for their porcelain were, by their nature, more plastic than those which we are able to employ in the West today, and to improve the workability of the theoretically equivalent recipe for Chinese porcelain of 50 per cent petuntse (feldspar + quartz) and 50 per cent kaolin (china clay), up to 5 per cent of bentonite or ball clay is often added.[24] Either the bentonite or the ball clay is generally substituted for up to 5 per cent of the quartz. Bentonite is a highly plastic colloidal clay of volcanic origin, and ball clay is a highly plastic sedimentary clay.

The making of porcelain is a very young craft indeed compared with the length of time that pottery of other sorts has been made. There had been pottery, much of it of extreme beauty and technical expertise, for something like 6000 years before the first porcelain was made in China. But it has been for a mere 270 years that hard-paste porcelain has been made at all in Europe, and in discovering how to do this in 1708 Germany was itself fifty years ahead of its rivals.

As far as can be ascertained, porcelain-making has never been a simple country craft. The materials cannot be dug locally and formed directly by country potters, like other clays. Neither can they be fired in simply constructed low-temperature kilns. It has always needed a great deal of knowledge, care and time to prepare the clay, and then it is a difficult and largely unco-operative material to handle compared with more plastic and malleable clays. Add to this the advanced kiln construction needed to obtain the high temperatures of at least $1280°C$ required to bring the clay to maturity and it will be seen that it has always been a technically advanced and refined process, making porcelain an expensive luxury for the few, rather than a simple and inexpensive product for everyday use.

The earliest porcelain made by the Chinese during the T'ang and Sung Dynasties has the fresh spontaneity of work made by potters who must have been responsible for the totality of a single piece, even though they were probably working as part of a large team. But by the time porcelain was well established and being produced for export, a vast network of both skilled and unskilled labour was generally employed to produce the final work. This was done by a succession of separate yet interdependent teams of workmen and skilled craftsmen. First there were the men who dug the kaolin and petuntse, then those who mixed, pulverized and refined it. Next there were the porters who carried their loads of raw materials, slung on the ends of long poles over their shoulders, down the mountainous paths and across rivers to the men who formed the pots. They then passed them to those who turned them, after which they were glazed by others, then decorated by specialists in decoration, and finally fired by kiln workers. They may have needed yet more decoration and firing by other groups of craftsmen if they were enamelled. Each stage was performed by skilled workmen and craftsmen, each working within his own circumscribed area of expertise.

These stages of subdivision of labour, many different hands going towards making one object, were the same in the eighteenth century when porcelain-making came to Europe, and the many groups of figure, bird and animal models were made in the same complex way. With these, there was not the same direct involvement with the clay by a potter as there was with the simpler figures and groups modelled directly in earthenware clay by potters working for a country market. Instead, the porcelain pieces, meant to grace the tables and homes of the rich and cultured, were composed by sculptors. They worked in some other more manageable material such as wax or wood, and then from these pieces of finished sculpture very complex moulds in many pieces were made by a master mould-maker. Into these the clay would be press-moulded or slip-cast. This method enabled the porcelain to take on forms which it would not have been possible to make by direct modelling in the raw material. The mind and eye behind the work would be that of a sculptor, not a potter, informed by a different set of skills and level of achievements, appealing to a different market than the more 'earthy' work of the earthenware pieces.

It is only very recently, through being backed up by the easy availability of factory-refined materials and high-temperature kilns, that a single potter working alone has been able to explore the possibilities of porcelain on the simple and sensually satisfying level of direct making that is offered by pinch-building and coiling, enjoying the complete experience of forming, decorating and firing it himself. A new tradition is being built up of hand-building in porcelain, using the very simplest making methods allied to the most sophisticated and refined materials and firing techniques.

Pots by Ruth Duckworth. ABOVE *Oval porcelain bowl, pinched, 6 inches high.* BELOW *A rugged stoneware pot, 12 inches high, partly glazed, made from folded slabs.*

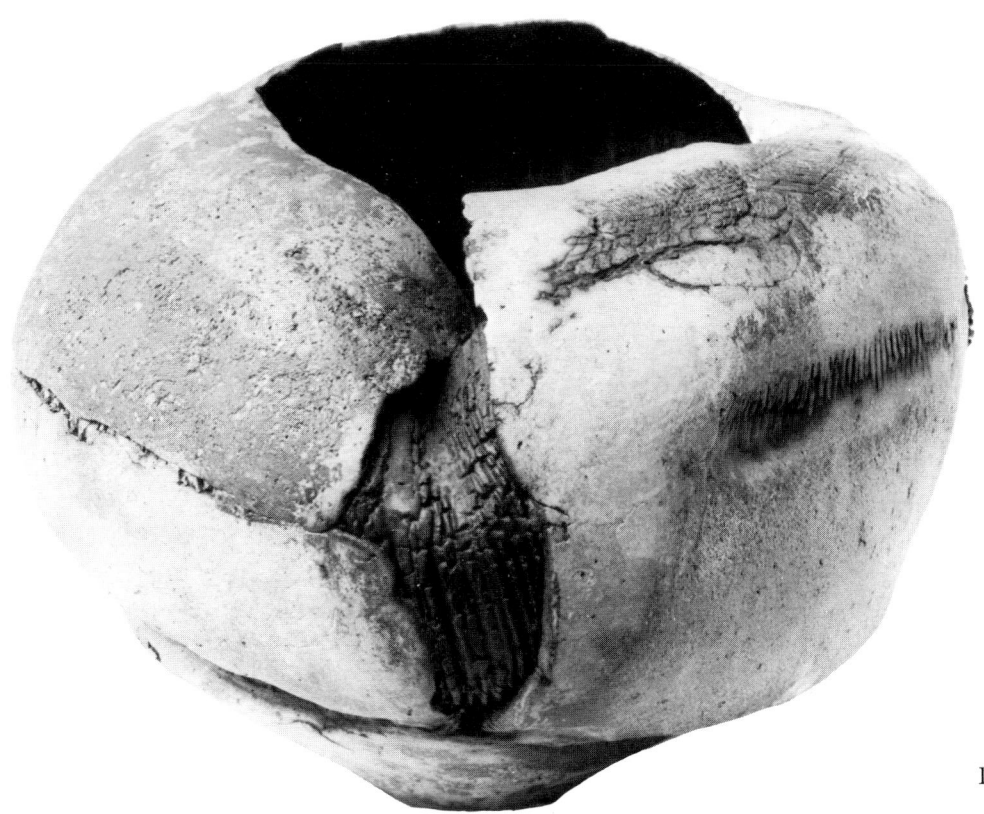

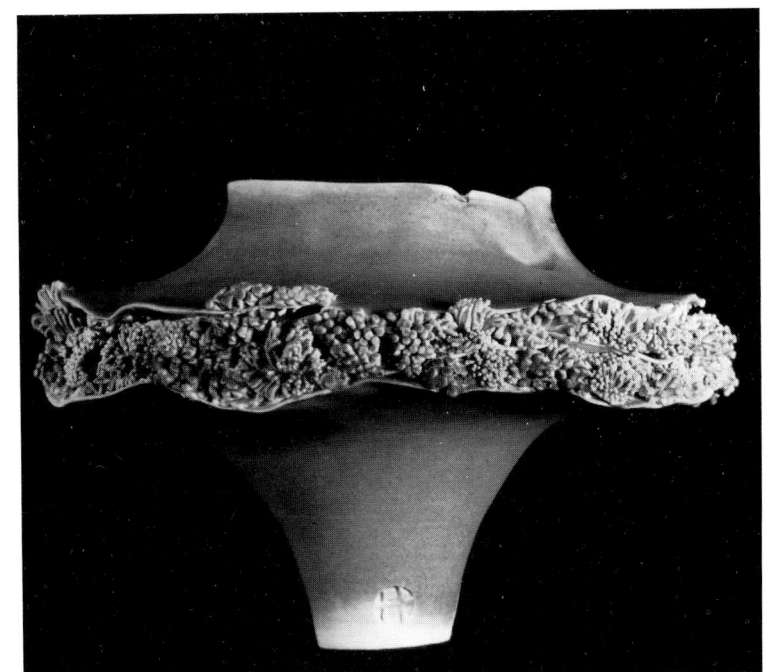

LEFT *Handbuilt stoneware bowls with painted slip decoration by Elizabeth Fritsch,* RIGHT *and* BELOW *Handbuilt porcelain by Peter Simpson. The pot on the right, 'Open Spinner', has extruded decoration in the sandwich.*

BELOW *Hand-modelled teapot by Jill Crowley. Raku fired.* RIGHT
Handmade bowls by John Ward, and BELOW *stoneware form by
Sheila Fournier.*

147

List of references

1. For mathematical and biological accounts of growth patterns and structures see: Peter S. Stevens, *Patterns in Nature* (Penguin Books, 1977); Adolf Portman, *Animal Forms and Patterns* (Faber & Faber, 1952); D'Arcy Wentworth Thompson, *On Growth and Form* (Cambridge University Press, 1942).
2. W. B. Honey, *Dresden China* (Faber & Faber, 1934), p. 23.
3. *The Travels of Marco Polo* (Everyman edition, Dent, 1967), p. 319.
4. Alan Smith, *Illustrated Guide to Liverpool Herculaneum Pottery, 1796–1840* (Barrie & Jenkins, 1970).
5. Soetsu Yanagi, *The Unknown Craftsman* (Kodansha International Ltd, Tokyo, Japan, 1972), p. 122.
6. *Larousse Encyclopaedia of the Earth* (Paul Hamlyn, 1965), p. 350.
7. William Burton, *Porcelain, its Art and Manufacture* (Batsford, 1906), pp. 98–9.
8. Rene A. Bravmann, *Open Frontiers: The Mobility of Art in Black Africa* (University of Washington Press, 1973), p. 16.
9. ibid, p. 82.
10. ibid, p. 14.
11. Sylvia Leith-Ross, *Ibo Pottery* (*Ceramic Review,* No. 51, London, 1978).
12. Sylvia Leith-Ross, *Nigerian Pottery* (Ibadan University Press, Nigeria, 1970), p. 161.
13. William Fagg and John Picton, *The Potter's Art in Africa* (Trustees of the British Museum, 1970), p. 8.
14. Fujio Koyama, *The Heritage of Japanese Ceramics* (Weatherhill and Tankasha, Tokyo, Japan, 1973).
15. For a full description of Kwali methods of making pottery see: Michael Cardew, *Pioneer Pottery* (Longman, 1969).
16. ibid.
17. Philip J. C. Dark, *Benin Art and Technology* (Clarendon Press, Oxford, 1973).
18. Robert M. Netting, *Pottery Making among the Kofyar,* see appendix to Sylvia Leith-Ross, *Nigerian Pottery* (Ibadan University Press, Nigeria, 1970).
19. See under 'Porcelain', *Oxford English Dictionary* (Clarendon Press, Oxford).
20. William Burton, *Porcelain, its Art and Manufacture* (Batsford, 1906), p. 17.
21. W. B. Honey, *Old English Porcelain* (Faber & Faber, 1977).
22. Walter A. Staehelin, *The Book of Porcelain* (Lund Humphries, 1966), p. 9.
23. Ixtlilxochitl, *Obras Históricas* (Mexico, 1891–2).
24. For further reading on this subject see Nigel Wood, *Oriental Glazes* (Pitman, London and Watson-Guptill, New York, 1978).

Bibliography

CHAPTER 1

Fujioka, Ryoichi *Shino and Oribe Ceramics* Shibundo Pub. Co., Tokyo 1970, Kodansha International Ltd, New York and San Francisco 1977

Leach, Bernard *Kenzan and his Tradition* Faber, London 1966

— *A Potter's Book* Faber, London 1945, Transatlantic Arts, New York 1973

Portmann, Adolf *Animal Forms and Patterns* Faber, 1952

Rawson, Philip *Ceramics* The Appreciation of the Arts Series, Oxford University Press 1971

Rhodes, Daniel *Pottery Form* Pitman, London 1978, Chilton, Philadelphia 1976

Sanders, Herbert H. *The World of Japanese Ceramics* Kodansha International Ltd, Tokyo 1967, Kodansha International USA Ltd, California

Searle, Patricia *Images from Life* British Museum Natural History Department, London 1971

Stevens, Peter S. *Patterns in Nature* Penguin Books, Harmondsworth 1977, Little, Brown, Boston 1974

Thompson, D'Arcy Wentworth *On Growth and Form* Cambridge University Press 1942, New York, First edition 1917

Valéry, Paul 'Man and the Sea Shell', in *Aesthetics* Routledge and Kegan Paul, London 1964

Yanagi, Soetsu *The Unknown Craftsman* Kodansha International, Tokyo 1972, Kodansha International USA Ltd, California, 1972

CHAPTERS 2 AND 3

Billington, Dora *The Technique of Pottery* rev. ed. by J. Colbeck, Batsford, London 1975

Birks, Tony *The Potter's Companion* Batsford, London 1977, E. P. Dutton, New York 1977

Casson, Michael *The Craft of the Potter* British Broadcasting Corporation, London 1977

Chappell, James *The Potters Complete Book of Clays and Glazes* Watson-Guptill, New York 1977

Conrad, John W. *Ceramic Formulas—The Complete Compendium* Macmillan Pub. Co. Inc., New York, 1973 and Collier Macmillan, London

Cooper, Emmanuel *Pottery* Macdonald, London 1976

— and Royle, Derek *Glazes for the Studio Potter* Batsford, London 1978

Fournier, Robert *Illustrated Dictionary of Practical Pottery* Van Nostrand Reinhold, New York and London 1973

Fraser, Harry *Glazes for the Craft Potter* Pitman, London 1973, Watson-Guptill, New York 1974

Grebanier, Joseph *Chinese Stoneware Glazes* Pitman, London, and Watson-Guptill, New York 1975

Hamer, Frank and Janet *Clays* Pitman, London 1978, Watson-Guptill, New York 1978

Leach, Bernard *A Potter's Book* Faber, London 1945, Transatlantic Arts, New York 1973

Lewenstein, Eileen and Cooper, Emmanuel (Eds) *Ceramic Review* The Craftsmen Potters Association of Great Britain

—*Glaze Recipes—200 Recipes from Practising Potters* enlarged and revised edition, C.P.A. 1978

Lynggaard, F. *Pottery: Raku Technique* Van Nostrand Reinhold, New York 1973

Rhodes, Daniel *Clay and Glazes for the Potter* Pitman, London 1962, Chilton, Philadelphia 1959

—*Stoneware and Porcelain* Pitman, London 1960, Chilton, Philadelphia 1959 and 1973

Shaw, Kenneth *Ceramic Colours and Pottery Decoration* MacLaren and Sons Ltd, London 1962

Wood, Nigel *Oriental Glazes* Pitman, London 1978, Watson-Guptill, New York 1978

CHAPTER 4

Bravmann, Rene A. *Open Frontiers—The Mobility of Art in Black Africa* University of Washington Press, Seattle and London 1973

Cardew, Michael *Pioneer Pottery* Longmans, Harlow 1969, St Martin's Press, New York 1971

Dark, Philip J. C. *An Introduction to Benin Art and Technology* Oxford Clarendon Press 1973

Fagg, William and Picton, John *The Potter's Art in Africa* British Museum Publication, London 1970

Gardi, René *African Crafts and Craftsmen* Van Nostrand Reinhold, New York 1969

Gonen, Rivka *Ancient Pottery* Cassells, London 1973

Hawkes, Nicolas 'Bassa Nge Pottery Technique' in Sylvia Leith-Ross *Nigerian Pottery* (see below)

Hodges, Henry *Technology in the Ancient World* Pelican Books 1971

Koyama, Fujio *The Heritage of Japanese Ceramics* Weatherhill / Tankasha, New York and Kyoto 1973

Leith-Ross, Sylvia *Nigerian Pottery* Ibadan University Press 1970

Netting, Robert M. 'Pottery-making among the Kofyar' in Sylvia Leith-Ross *Nigerian Pottery* (see above)

Riegger, H. *Primitive Pottery* Van Nostrand Reinhold, New York 1973

Trowell, Margaret *African Design* Faber, London 1960

Also of interest are frequent articles on traditional methods of hand-building in *Ceramic Review*, the bi-monthly magazine published by the Craftsmen Potters Association of Great Britain, and edited by Eileen Lewenstein and Emmanuel Cooper. For example:

No. 13 Jan/Feb 1972 'Pottery-making in Zambia' by Giselle Underhill

No. 20 March/April 1973 'A Visit to a Pottery Village in West Africa' by Tanya Dobbs

No. 27 May/June 1974 'Maya Potters of Southern Belize' by Deborah Hughes Hallett

No. 28 July/August 1974 'Pueblo Pottery of the North American Indian' by Val Barry

No. 29 Sept/Oct 1974 'Traditional Pottery in India' by S. K. Mirmira

No. 34 July/Aug 1975 'Abuja after Michael Cardew' by Michael O'Brien

No. 36 Nov/Dec 1975 'The Potters of La Arena, Panama' by Vronwy Hankey

No. 48 Nov/Dec 1977 'Potters of Bauchi Town, Nigeria' by Jonathan Slye

No. 51 May/June 1978 'Ibo Pottery' by Sylvia Leith-Ross
The bi-monthly magazine of the Crafts Advisory Committee, *Crafts*, has many articles of interest, e.g.:

No. 34 Sept/Oct 1978 'A Berber Potter' by Jennifer Balfour-Paul

CHAPTER 5

Burton, William *Porcelain, its Nature, Art and Manufacture* Batsford, London 1906

Charleston, J. (ed.) *World Ceramics* Paul Hamlyn, Feltham 1968

Cushion, John P. *Animals in Pottery and Porcelain* Studio Vista, London 1974

Godden, Geoffrey *Godden's Guide to English Porcelain* Granada 1978, London and New York

Honey, W. B. *Old English Porcelain* Bell, London 1931, new edition 1977

Lane, Arthur *English Porcelain Figures of the Eighteenth Century* Faber, London 1961

Medley, Margaret *The Chinese Potter* Phaidon, Oxford, and Scribners, New York 1976

Osborne, Harold (ed.) *The Oxford Companion to the Decorative Arts* Oxford Clarendon Press 1975

Reeve, John 'Notes on Porcelain' *Pottery Quarterly*, Nos 43 and 44

Rhodes, Daniel *Stoneware and Porcelain* Pitman, London 1960, Chilton, Philadelphia 1959

Sandeman, Alison *Working with Porcelain* Pitman, London, and Watson-Guptill, New York 1979

Savage, George *Eighteenth-century Porcelain* Spring Books, London 1964

Staehelin, Walter A. *The Book of Porcelain* Benteli-Verlag, Bern 1965, Lund Humphries, London 1966

Wood, Nigel 'Chinese Porcelain' *Pottery Quarterly*, No. 47, Vol. 12

Wood, Nigel *Oriental Glazes* Pitman, London, and Watson-Guptill, New York 1978